A ROUND OF
BOXING

A ROUND OF BOXING

BOXING

A TRIP THROUGH TIME

RALPH OATES

FONTHILL

Fonthill Media Language Policy

Fonthill Media publishes in the international English language market. One language edition is published worldwide. As there are minor differences in spelling and presentation, especially with regard to American English and British English, a policy is necessary to define which form of English to use. The Fonthill Policy is to use the form of English native to the author. Ralph Oates was born and educated in the United Kingdom; therefore, British English has been adopted in this publication.

Fonthill Media Limited
Fonthill Media LLC
www.fonthillmedia.com
office@fonthillmedia.com

First published in the United Kingdom and the United States of America 2019

British Library Cataloguing in Publication Data:
A catalogue record for this book is available from the British Library

Copyright © Ralph Oates 2019

ISBN 978-1-78155-692-4

Typeset in 10.5pt on 13pt Sabon
Printed and bound in England

Foreword

I have been involved in boxing for a number of years in various capacities as a boxer, trainer, applied sports psychologists, manager, and British Boxing Board of Control inspector. In my time, I have met some amazing boxers from around the world, many of whom I can count as friends. So I think I can humbly say that I know a little something about the sport. I won the British featherweight championship in 1991, stopping defending title-holder Sean Murphy in round five, which understandably was the greatest night of my career. I was pleased when Ralph Oates asked me to write a foreword for his latest book, *A Round of Boxing*.

Over the years, boxing has given the sport some magnificent fighters in many weight divisions from minimum to heavyweight. In this book, Ralph has produced some interesting facts in an easy to read way, which I am sure will intrigue the followers of the sport.

My first-ever literary contact with boxing was at around twelve when I read a short story on the former heavyweight world champion Gene Tunney. This particular story was not about the physical aspect of boxing but the cerebral psychological activities prior to the big fight and boy did Gene Tunney have a fight on his hands against Jack 'The Manassa Mauler' Dempsey. This story told of Gene relaxing, playing chess, and reading poetry during his training. Gene's fight preparation was ridiculed by the fight media and fans alike. He was not given a ghost of a chance against Dempsey, who had utterly destroyed just about every opponent he had faced in a world title fight. The rest is history, as Tunney went on to comfortably outpoint Dempsey over ten rounds, not just once but twice. Reading this as a youngster left an indelible mark on me, which in turn became part of my resilience against adversity later on in my boxing career.

Ralph Oates, being a former amateur boxer himself, knows how to string shots together as well as words. We have had many an in-depth talk on boxing over the years. These talks go on for many enjoyable hours, which brings us to the irrefragable fact that although, with the noble art of boxing you may exhaust yourself, you can never exhaust the subject. I always look forward to reading about Ralph's books on boxing as he has such a great slick style in his writing that is interesting, intelligent, and a joy to read. Your hardest fight ever will be trying to find a better book. *A Round of Boxing* is a superb knowledgeable read from the first round to the last.

Gary 'Dynamite' De'Roux
Former featherweight champion of Great Britain, 1991

Acknowledgements

My personal thanks to Howard Oates for his keen assistance in helping to check the information in the book—no easy task.

I also dedicate the book to the memory of Ruby Oates, who was a very special lady.

A very big thank you to my very good friend former British featherweight champion Gary De'Roux for taking the time to pen the foreword for the book. The photographs that appear in the book are courtesy of Derek Rowe, Philip Sharkey, and Les Clark. Sadly, Les passed away in 2015, thus his wife Jackie Clark kindly gave me her permission to use said images. Finally, many thanks to both Jamie Hardwick and Jay Slater of Fonthill Media for their hard work and guidance during the production of the book.

Please note: The Commonwealth Championship in bygone years was known as the Empire title. However, I have used the term 'Commonwealth' throughout the book for simplicity.

Contents

Weight Divisions in the Professional Ranks

Minimumweight/Strawweight	105 lb
Light-flyweight	108 lb
Flyweight	112 lb
Super-flyweight	115 lb
Bantamweight	118 lb
Super-bantamweight	122 lb
Featherweight	126 lb
Super-featherweight	130 lb
Lightweight	135 lb
Super-lightweight	140 lb
Welterweight	147 lb
Super-welterweight	154 lb
Middleweight	160 lb
Super-middleweight	168 lb
Light-heavyweight	175 lb
Cruiserweight	200 lb
Heavyweight	200 lb and over

World Boxing Organisations

EBU	European Boxing Union
IBA	International Boxing Association
IBF	International Boxing Federation
IBO	International Boxing Organisation
IBU	International Boxing Union
UBF	Universal Boxing Federation
WBA	World Boxing Association
WBC	World Boxing Council
WBO	World Boxing Organisation
WBU	World Boxing Union
WIBF	Women's International Boxing Federation

Introduction

I am not really sure when I first became interested in boxing—at least I have not got the exact date or time. I know I was at school and that I was not exactly a star football player or indeed a budding cricketer. These two sports held very little interest for me. I casually followed boxing and read the reports about various fights that had taken place in the UK and all over the world. I was really intrigued about the men who took part inside the square ring and had an admiration for their courage and respective skills. I did not then realise or even think about the politics that play a big part in the sport; that knowledge would come later.

My actual involvement in boxing came about when the sports master at my school put me in to spar with a boy who was an experienced boxer. To a certain extent, I resented it since I appeared to have no say in the matter, but, strangely, I also welcomed it as, deep down, I always wanted to have a go, so to speak. To that teacher's surprise, and certainly the boy I exchanged blows with, I did rather well; in fact, I got the better of him in the sparring, which at times became a little heated. The trainer was so impressed that he encouraged me to continue and hence fight in full contests, which I did for a couple of years with a degree of success, winning thirty-seven of my forty bouts. My amateur boxing career came to an end later when I became short-sighted. Was I a loss to the boxing world? I do not think so. I was good at the level I was fighting at, but when the time came for me to step up another level (and that time would eventually come), it might well have been a different story. In truth, I think it might very well have been.

After I departed from active involvement in the ring, I continued to follow the sport. I was unable to get away from it. I believe anyone involved in the sport never escapes it; they get drawn back in one capacity or another.

I read everything about boxing I could find, following all championship fights, whether world, European, British, and Commonwealth (then called Empire) bouts. I would also take note of the contenders and the newcomers in the UK, the USA, and many other parts of the world. Over the years, I made notes of the many events that had taken place inside the ring or bouts that produced unusual situations or facts of interest.

While I consider boxing to be a great sport on so many levels, it is apparent that many others do not feel the same. Everyone knows that boxing has to defend itself from time to time against those who dislike the sport with a passion and would like to see it banned, calling it brutal and dangerous. Life can be brutal and is most certainly dangerous. Fuel is thus added to the argument of the 'ban the boxing brigade' when, on occasion, a fighter suffers a fatality or is badly hurt during a contest. I will not go into personalities or the bouts in question since such events have been well-documented over the years. I will say that when one considers the number of fights that take place all over the world, serious injuries are thankfully few and far between. On saying that, I would agree without reservation that even one serious injury is far too many; there is no argument about that. We have to face the truth: boxing is a dangerous sport and it would be naïve to think otherwise; everyone who steps into the square ring knows that. To their credit, the various boxing organisations who run the sport have continuously come up with ways to make the sport safer and continue to do so. I could, of course, come up with the well-worn defence that many other sports are dangerous—some far more indeed than boxing. Such a statement is true, and when a fatality or serious injury takes place in those sports, we do not see anyone banging the drum and calling for a ban.

However, despite various critics, the sport survives and continues to turn out interesting personalities who capture the imagination of those who follow the sport and often entices new enthusiasts. Participants from various weight divisions who are ranked with the greats include the legendary Joe Louis, Rocky Marciano, Muhammad Ali, Joe Frazier, Henry Armstrong, Sugar Ray Robinson Roberto Duran, and in more modern times Floyd Mayweather Jr.

A Round of Boxing chronicles a selection of facts that I feel will be of interest to followers of the sport. The facts have developed in the ring over the years and there have been some interesting facts, that is for sure; these include, for example, the tallest man to hold a version of the world heavyweight title, the fastest win in a world flyweight championship, the first fighter to win the British super-welterweight crown, and the only British fighter to win three Lonsdale Belts outright. These and many other facts are presented in chronological order in a way that allows the reader to dip in anywhere in the book to find a factoid. I do hope the reader will enjoy the book and find it to be a knockout read.

1

Round One:
1891–1929

British-born Bob Fitzsimmons became the first man to capture a world championship in three different weight divisions. Fitzsimmons accomplished this feat by first winning the world middleweight title, knocking out Irish-born Nonpareil Jack Dempsey in round thirteen in a fight to the finish on 14 January 1891 at the Olympic Club in New Orleans, Louisiana. The second championship came at heavyweight when Fitzsimmons knocked out American title-holder James J. Corbett in round fourteen in a fight to the finish on 17 March 1897 at the Race Track Arena in Carson City, Nevada. Then on 25 November 1903, he added the light-heavyweight crown to his collection when he outpointed defending champion George Gardner of America over twenty rounds at Mechanics Pavilion in San Francisco in California.

Everything in the course of time changes sometimes for the best, sometimes for the worst; boxing is no exception to that rule. On 7 September 1892, a new era in boxing started when James J. Corbett fought fellow American John L. Sullivan in a contest for the world heavyweight title. This was the first bout in the division to be fought under the Marquess of Queensbury rules: an important change in the fight game, which looked like being for the best. The contest that took place at the Olympic Club in New Orleans, Louisiana, saw Corbett crowned the new champion when he knocked out Sullivan in round twenty-one in a fight to the finish.

On 22 April 1903, in what is considered to be the first-ever world light-heavyweight title bout to be staged saw Jack Root, who was born in the Czech Republic, outpoint American Charles Kid McCoy over ten rounds to claim the respective crown. The contest took place at the Light Guard

Armoury in Detroit, Michigan. The referee of this contest was notable since he was none other than western legend Bat Masterson.

American Oliver Kirk achieved an outstanding feat at the 1904 Olympic Games, one which is not likely to be equalled again, when he won two gold medals at the same event: one was captured at featherweight when he outpointed countryman Frank Haller and later at bantamweight whereupon he stopped another fellow American, George Finnegan, in the third round. In modern times, a boxer would not be allowed to compete in two weight divisions at the same games.

It was the future meeting the past on 17 July 1907 when American Jack Johnson (the future world heavyweight champion) met England's Bob Fitzsimmons (the former world heavyweight title-holder). The two fighters squared off at Washington Sporting Club in Philadelphia, Pennsylvania. The contest was scheduled for six rounds but was brought to its final conclusion in the second session when Johnson knocked out Fitzsimmons.

On 2 December 1907, the National Sporting Club in Covent Garden, London, hosted the first world heavyweight title bout to be staged in the UK. The champion Tommy Burns of Canada was putting his championship on the line against Britain's Gunner Moir. If expectations were high for a British win, they were soon dashed when Burns retained his crown by a knockout in round ten of a contest scheduled for twenty.

American Jack Johnson gave himself a belated and much-wanted Christmas present on 26 December 1908 when at the Sydney Stadium in New South Wales, Australia, he stopped Canada's defending world heavyweight champion Tommy Burns in round fourteen in a bout scheduled for twenty. This was an important milestone in boxing since Johnson became the first African American to win this crown. Johnson had been chasing this title for some considerable time and it did look at times as if his desire to step into the ring and fight for this crown would prove to be futile.

Freddie Welsh from Wales punched his way to the British lightweight championship on 8 November 1909, outpointing holder Johnny Summers over twenty rounds. The contest took place at the National Sporting Club in Covent Garden, London. Welsh had the distinction of being the first man in the division to be presented with the National Sporting Club's Lonsdale Belt.

Percy Jones became the first Welsh boxer to win a world crown in the professional ranks when he outpointed England's defending champion Bill Ladbury over twenty rounds on 26 January 1914 to capture the IBU version of the flyweight title at the National Sporting Club in Covent Garden. Jones also won the British and European title in this contest.

American Al McCoy wasted no time in becoming the first boxer with a southpaw stance to win the world middleweight title. On 7 April 1914,

McCoy quickly found the range and landed the winning punch to knock out fellow countryman and defending champion George Chip in the opening round. The contest was staged at the Broadway SC in Brooklyn, New York, and was scheduled for ten rounds.

American Harry Stone proved to be a very busy fighter since in the space of eight days he took part in three bouts to be fought over the duration of twenty rounds in Australia; the first of these took place at the Sydney Stadium in New South Wales against Australian Herb (Kid McCoy) on 22 April 1916. Stone emerged the victor on points. Then, at the same venue on 24 April 1916, Stone lost a points decision to Tommy Uren of Australia. Then on 29 April 1916, Stone stepped into the ring at the Brisbane Stadium in Queensland to confront French fighter Fernand Quendreux and won the battle when his opponent retired in round fifteen.

During his long boxing career, Len Harvey won the British and Commonwealth middleweight, British and Commonwealth light-heavyweight plus world light-heavyweight (British version), and British and Commonwealth heavyweight championships. Harvey participated in 146 bouts (winning 122, losing fourteen, and drawing ten of said engagements). Harvey had his first professional contest on 2 January 1920 at the Cosmopolitan Gymnasium in Plymouth, Devon, outpointing Young King over six rounds. It could be said that Harvey made an early start to his professional career: he was aged just twelve years, five months, and twenty-two days.

On 18 November 1921, Italian-born Johnny Dundee met American opponent George KO Chaney at Madison Square Garden, New York. Dundee had his arm lifted aloft when he defeated Chaney by a disqualification in round five of fifteen. This was a special occasion as this contest was for the inaugural world super-featherweight title as recognised in New York.

On 17 March 1923, Ireland's Mike McTigue captured the world light-heavyweight title from Senegalese Battling Siki at the La Scala Theatre in Dublin, Ireland. It was not an easy night's work since McTigue had to travel the full twenty rounds to get the points decision. This title fight made it into the record books as it was the last world championship fight in this weight category to go the said distance of twenty rounds.

American Tommy Gibbons clashed in a contest scheduled for twenty rounds against Londoner Jack Bloomfield on 9 August 1924. The heavyweight bout was over in the third stanza, with Gibbons winning by virtue of a knockout. This was the first boxing contest to be staged at Wembley Stadium in London.

Most individuals find Flowers to be a delight; however, you might very well have been given an argument about that fact from Harry Greb and with good reason too. On 26 February 1926, Tiger Flowers won the world middleweight title at Madison Square Garden in New York when he outpointed defending champion and fellow countryman Harry Greb over the duration of fifteen rounds. In so doing, Flowers became the first African American to hold this championship.

Teddy Baldock outpointed American Archie Bell over fifteen rounds on 5 May 1927 at the Royal Albert Hall in Kensington, London, to win the vacant British version of the world bantamweight crown. At the age of nineteen years, eleven months, and eleven days, Baldock became the youngest British boxer at the time to win a world championship in the professional ranks.

On 25 February 1928, the reigning British and Commonwealth light-heavyweight champion Gipsy Daniels ventured to Germany; his task was to take on Max Schmeling. The engagement looked to be a difficult one, indeed a match that looked likely to add a defeat to his record. However, the trip was not doomed for failure since he scored his best ever victory in the professional ranks. At the Festhalle, Frankfurt, he provided a shock when he knocked out Max Schmeling in the opening session in a bout scheduled for ten rounds. This was a return contest between the Welshman and the German since on 2 December 1927, Schmeling had outpointed Daniels over ten rounds at the Sportpalast in Schoenberg, Berlin. It appeared that Daniels was determined that he would not let the fight go to the scorecard in their second meeting. In the fullness of time, Schmeling went on to win the vacant NBA and NYSAC world heavyweight title on 12 June 1930, defeating American Jack Sharkey by a four-round disqualification at the Yankee Stadium, New York, in a contest set for the duration of fifteen rounds. Then, when a former world champion, he became the first man to defeat future great Joe Louis by a knockout in round twelve of fifteen on 19 June 1936 at the same venue in the USA.

On 18 April 1929, Emile Pladner of France lost his NBA/IBU world flyweight crown in his first defence at the Velodrome d'Hiver in Paris against American Frankie Genaro by a disqualification in round five of a contest set for fifteen. The infringement was that Pladner landed a low left hook. Thus, at the time, Pladner created the dubious record of holding the title for the shortest period of time in the division: just forty-seven days. Pladner had taken the crown by a knockout over Genaro in the first round of a bout scheduled for fifteen on 2 March 1929 at the same venue in France.

Panama Al Brown, a highly skilled fighter, won the vacant NYSAC version of the world bantamweight title on 18 June 1929 when he outpointed Spanish-born Gregorio Vidal over fifteen rounds. The contest, which took place at the Queensboro Stadium, Long Island, saw Brown become Panama's (and indeed Latin America's) first world boxing champion.

On 24 November 1929, Nipper Pat Daly won a fifteen-round points decision over his opponent Jim Briley at the Premierland in Whitechapel, London. Daly had been a most active fighter during the year, participating in an astonishing thirty-three bouts of which he won twenty-nine, lost three, and drew one.

In 1929, the British Boxing Board of Control was formed, thus taking over from the National Sporting Club, which had controlled the sport since 1891.

2

Round Two:
1930–1939

On 12 June 1930, Max Schmeling and American Jack Sharkey stepped into the ring at the Yankee Stadium in New York to contest the vacant NBA and NYSAC world heavyweight crown. The championship ended in a most unexpected way when Sharkey was disqualified in the fourth session in a bout scheduled for fifteen rounds. Sharkey was deemed to have landed a low blow against his opponent. This was the first time in the division's rich history for a world heavyweight title fight to end with a disqualification. Schmeling also became the first boxer from Germany to win this title.

Tunisia saw its first world champion crowned in the professional ranks on 26 October 1931 when Young Perez captured the NBA and IBU world flyweight titles, knocking out defending holder Frankie Genaro in two rounds of a scheduled fifteen. The contest took place in France at the Palais des Sports in Paris.

American fighters George Nichols and Dave Maier fought it out on 18 March 1932 for the vacant NBA version of the world light-heavyweight championship at the Chicago Stadium, in Illinois. The contest went the full distance of ten rounds, at the end of which Nichols was crowned the new title-holder when given the points decision. Nichols became the first boxer with the southpaw stance to hold a version of the title at the poundage.

It was an intriguing battle of the two Maxes on 8 June 1933 at the Yankee Stadium in New York when future world heavyweight king Max Baer of the USA swapped punches with the then former world heavyweight champion Max Schmeling of Germany. Baer was the fighter on the ascendancy and was expected to take the win. Baer showed that he had genuine championship potential when he emerged the victor, stopping Schmeling in round ten of fifteen.

Primo Carnera became the first Italian-born boxer to win the world heavyweight crown on 29 June 1933 at the Madison Square Garden Bowl in Long Island City in Queens, New York. Carnera accomplished the task when he knocked out the defending NYSAC and NBA title-holder Jack Sharkey of America in round six of fifteen. Not only did Carnera win the championship but he gained revenge for a previous loss that he had suffered against Sharkey in a bout, which had taken place on 12 October 1931. On that occasion at Ebbet's Field in Brooklyn, Sharkey had outpointed Carnera over the duration of fifteen rounds.

Barney Ross of America defended his world super-lightweight crown against countryman Frankie Klick at the Civic Auditorium, San Francisco, on 5 March 1934. The contest went the full ten rounds and for the first time in the weight division, a world title fight concluded with a draw.

On 1 June 1935, at the Plaza de Toros de Valencia in Spain, Baltazar Sangchili captured the IBU version of the world bantamweight title when he outpointed defending champion Panama Al Brown over fifteen rounds. In defeating the Panamanian-born title-holder, Baltazar became the first Spanish professional boxer to win a world crown in the professional ranks.

At Madison Square Garden in New York, on 20 December 1935, Jock McAvoy served up a shock for reigning NBA and NYSAC world middleweight title-holder Eddie (Babe) Risko of America and thus revealed that he was not a man to be taken lightly. McAvoy was nicknamed the 'Rochdale Thunder Bolt' and Risko must have felt he had been hit by a thunderbolt when he felt the full power of the Briton's punch in no uncertain terms; the American was shockingly knocked out in the first round. The contest was a non-title bout scheduled for ten rounds. It was lucky for Risko that he did not have his title on the line against the hard-punching Briton on the night. A return bout looked to be the order of the day this time, with the championship being at stake. McAvoy, however, was not granted the return with the American for the respective title—a case of once bitten twice shy.

The Val Barker Trophy is awarded to the boxer at the Olympic Games who is considered to have been the most stylish. Val Barker was a British amateur heavyweight boxer and president of the ABA; the trophy was thus dedicated in his honour. The first recipient of the trophy was American flyweight bronze medal winner Louis Laurie at the 1936 Berlin games.

John Henry Lewis became the first American holder of the world light-heavyweight crown to defend the title in Britain. The event took place on 9 November 1936 at the Empire Pool in Wembley, London. Homegrown challenger Len Harvey used his considerable boxing skills in his attempt to win the crown but failed in his bid, losing a fifteen-round points decision.

American Henry Armstrong (nicknamed 'Homicide Hank') is a fighter whose name truly belongs with the greats to have graced the sport over the years; there can be little if any doubt about that fact as Armstrong had a truly incredible career inside the square ring. Armstrong won the NYSAC and NBA version of the world featherweight crown on 29 October 1937 at Madison Square Garden in New York, knocking out holder Petey Sarron in round six of a scheduled fifteen. At the time, Armstrong was the holder of the Mexican and Californian version of the championship. Armstrong went for the second world title number when, on 31 May 1938, he entered the ring at MSG Bowl in Long Island to challenge fellow countryman Barney Ross for the welterweight crown. Ross was a good champion but after fifteen rounds of boxing Armstrong proved that he was the better man and was crowned the new title-holder when awarded the points decision. On 17 August 1938, Armstrong stepped down to lightweight to challenge that division's world title-holder in the shape of Lou Ambers of the USA at Madison Square Garden in New York. It might have appeared that the duel title-holder was pushing his luck. Once again, Armstrong did the unbelievable when he emerged victorious with a fifteen-round points decision. In so doing, Armstrong made boxing history by becoming the first man to simultaneously hold three world titles. Armstrong later gave up the featherweight crown.

Jock McAvoy made a valiant attempt to capture the British light-heavyweight crown from reigning champion Len Harvey on 10 July 1939. McAvoy was outpointed over fifteen rounds by Harvey on 7 April 1938 at the Harringay Arena, London, in his first bid for this crown. The second challenge by McAvoy, which took place at the White City Stadium, London, also involved the vacant Commonwealth light-heavyweight crown and was also billed as for the vacant British Boxing Board of Control's vacant world light-heavyweight title. The championship fight went the full fifteen rounds and saw Harvey the victor on points. It was notable that the fight created, at the time, a post-war record attendance of a reported 90,000 spectators.

While Harvey was given recognition as world champion in the light-heavyweight division by the BBB of C, he had a very strong rival in the shape of American Billy Conn, who captured a large chunk of the fragmented championship. At Madison Square Garden on 13 July 1939, Conn won the vacant NBA crown and also captured the NYSAC version from defending king and fellow countryman Melio Bettina, whom he outpointed over fifteen rounds.

Eric Boon became the first boxer in the lightweight division to win a British Boxing Board of Control Lonsdale Belt outright for winning three British title bouts. Boon acquired this distinction on 9 December 1939 when at the Harringay Arena in London, he knocked out challenger and former champion Dave Crowley in round seven for the title in a bout slated for fifteen. Boon had won the championship from Crowley on 15 December 1938 at the same venue by a thirteen-round knockout in a bout once again set for fifteen. In between the two bouts with Crowley, Boon had made a successful first defence against challenger Arthur Danahar who failed to last the scheduled fifteen rounds when stopped in the fourteenth session. The bout with Danahar took place on 23 February 1939 and, once again, the venue on that occasion was the Harringay Arena.

3

Round Three:
1940–1949

At the Bulkeley Stadium in Hartford, Connecticut, on 25 July 1940, two fighters made their professional debut: Joey Marcus and Willie Pep; they were to engage in a contest scheduled for four rounds. Pep won the bout and would go on from this victory to be ranked with the greats of the featherweight division. Pep twice won the world crown in said division and accumulated a record of 241 fights (winning 229, losing eleven, and drawing one). Pep had his last contest on 16 March 1966, losing a six-round points verdict to Calvin Woodland at the City Arena in Richmond, Virginia. Needless to say, this was not the boxing master of old; Pep in his prime would have given a boxing lesson to Woodland. Pep was inducted into the International Boxing Hall of Fame in 1990. Pep sadly passed away on 23 November 2006, aged eighty-four years, two months, and four days.

Future world welterweight and middleweight world title-holder Sugar Ray Robinson was a natural-born fighter, defeating every man who faced him in the ring. Robinson truly looked a little special—a master of his trade. It was getting to be a foregone conclusion that every time this gifted exponent of the noble art stepped between the ropes to ply his trade, the outcome would be the same: a sure-fire victory for him. However, Robinson did not find it so sweet when he met an unexpected roadblock and hence had his undefeated professional record snapped in his forty-first outing. The setback took place on 5 February 1943 against future world middleweight champion Jake LaMotta. LaMotta was one hard man to do battle with, but it looked as if Robinson would have no problem in continuing his winning run when matched against him. LaMotta was no respecter of reputations and had not come to lie down or surrender meekly to the man in front of him. LaMotta provided the shock when he employed the right tactics to outpoint Robinson over ten rounds at the Olympia Stadium in Detroit, Michigan. Robinson had previously outpointed LaMotta over ten rounds on 2 October 1942 at Madison Square Garden in New York.

On 19 June 1943, Scotland's Jackie Paterson stepped into the ring at Hampden Park in Glasgow to defend his British and Empire flyweight titles and also challenge England's Peter Kane for the British and New York version of the world flyweight championship. Paterson gave his many fans in attendance plenty to cheer about when he proved successful by knocking out Kane in the first round of fifteen. The Scot hence became the first man in the division to win a version of the world crown with the southpaw stance.

Juan Zurita boxed his way to a fifteen-round points decision over holder Sammy Angott of America to capture the NBA world lightweight crown at the Gilmore Field, Los Angeles. The contest that took place on 8 March 1944 saw Zurita become the first Mexican to hold a version of the world championship in this division.

When Bos Murphy entered the ring on 26 January 1948 to contest the vacant Commonwealth middleweight title with British Champion Vince Hawkins, it had all the makings of being a good scrap between two highly motivated fighters. The title was a very valuable asset to have and a sure-fire help to ensure more lucrative matches in the future. Now if you were pushed to pick a winner, you would lean towards Hawkins—a much more accomplished boxer with a wealth of experience on his side. The Briton had a ledger that comprised seventy-six fights with seventy-two wins, three defeats, and one draw, and had shared the ring with better company. Now, in comparison, Murphy's record was twenty-one bouts with three defeats and he was boxing away from home in Hawkins' backyard. At the Royal Albert Hall in London, a shock result took place when Murphy produced the goods and took a fifteen-round points decision to take the championship and become the first New Zealand-born boxer to win the Commonwealth title in this division since Bill Heffernan, who reigned from 1894–1896.

Dick Turpin won the British middleweight title on 28 June 1948 when he outpointed holder Vince Hawkins over fifteen rounds for the championship at Villa Park in Birmingham. Turpin became on this occasion the first black boxer to win a British title. On that night, Turpin was also defending his Commonwealth championship, which he duly held. Turpin had won the Commonwealth title when he knocked out holder Bos Murphy of New Zealand in the first round of a contest set for fifteen at the Highfield Road in Coventry on 18 May 1948.

Freddie Mills put on a great performance to give his career and British boxing a boost when he fought his way to the world light-heavyweight title at the White City Stadium in London on 26 July 1948. Mills duly won the crown, outpointing the reigning title-holder Gus Lesnevich of America over fifteen rounds. If you had to pick a winner prior to the bout and did not let your heart rule your head, you would have to go for Lesnevich to retain the crown. The two fighters had crossed gloves previously on 14 May 1946 at the Harringay Arena, London, whereupon the fighter from the USA kept the title, stopping his brave challenger in round ten of a contest set for fifteen. It looked as if Lesnevich would repeat the victory in their second meeting but Mills more than rose to the occasion to emerge a good victor on the night.

During his career, American Jake LaMotta won the world middleweight crown from a European boxer in the shape of Marcel Cerdan of France on 16 June 1949. The Frenchman retired in round nine of fifteen at the Briggs Stadium in Detroit, Michigan. After that, LaMotta had declared war on the leading European middleweights. The first defence by LaMotta came against Italian Tiberio Mitri on 12 July 1950 at Madison Square Garden in New York; on this occasion, LaMotta retained the crown on points over fifteen rounds. At the Olympia Stadium in Detroit, on 13 September 1950, Frenchman Laurent Dauthuille stepped in with LaMotta. Dauthuille was not able to gain revenge for fellow countryman Cerdan and return the title to France has he hoped. The rugged American was all over his challenger and remained king of the hill when he retained his crown by knocking out his challenger in round fifteen. LaMotta finally lost the championship to fellow American Sugar Ray Robinson on 14 February 1951 at the Chicago Stadium in Illinois when stopped in the thirteenth round of a scheduled fifteen.

American Sandy Saddler won the vacant NBA world super-featherweight crown on 6 December 1949 when he outpointed Orlando Zulueta of Cuba over ten rounds at the Arena in Cleveland, Ohio. This was the first world title bout to be staged at the poundage since 25 December 1933 when the then-defending title-holder, Kid Chocolate of Cuba, was stopped in the seventh round of fifteen by American challenger Frankie Klick at the Arena in Philadelphia, Pennsylvania. Klick did not defend the crown, hence the championship remained dormant with very little interest given to the championship in this division until the respective Saddler–Zulueta match-up.

4

Round Four:
1950–1959

On 24 April 1950, Albert Finch was successful in his bid for the British middleweight championship when he outpointed title-holder Dick Turpin over fifteen rounds. The bout took place at the Ice Rink, Nottingham. This was Finch's second crack at the crown as on 20 June 1949, he went up against Turpin for not only the domestic title but also the Commonwealth championship at the St Andrews Birmingham City FC in the West Midlands and came up short, losing a fifteen-round points decision. Finch did not reign for too long since in his first defence, he faced yet another Turpin: Dick's younger brother Randolph. At the Harringay Arena, on 17 October 1950, Turpin won the crown and gained revenge for his older brother's defeat when he knocked out Finch in round five of a scheduled fifteen.

On 2 December 1950, British bantamweight title-holder Danny O'Sullivan travelled to Wembley Stadium in Gauteng, Johannesburg, to challenge South Africa's Vic Toweel for the world and Commonwealth bantamweight crown. O'Sullivan bravely failed in his attempt when stopped in round ten of a fifteen contest. During the course of the fight, O'Sullivan was floored fourteen times, creating at the time a record number of knockdowns in a world championship contest.

Sugar Ray Robinson, a former world welterweight champion, first won the undisputed world middleweight title on 14 February 1951 when he stopped the reigning champion Jake LaMotta in round thirteen of a contest set for fifteen. The venue the two Americans fought at was the Chicago Stadium, Illinois. Robinson lost the crown in his first defence to England's Randolph Turpin on 10 July 1951 at Earls Court Arena, Kensington, by a fifteen-round points decision. In a quickly arranged return, Robinson regained the title by stopping Turpin in round ten in a bout scheduled for fifteen on 12 September 1951 at the Polo Grounds in New York. After two successful defences of the championship and a failed attempt at the world light-heavyweight crown, Robinson announced his retirement from the sport in December 1952. In 1955, Robinson made a return to boxing and after six bouts (of which he won five and lost one), he once again set his sights on the world middleweight title, held by Hawaii-born Carlo (Bobo) Olson. Robinson once again proved his greatness when he regained the crown, knocking out Olson in round two on 9 December 1955. It seemed obvious from the get-go that the contest would not go the full fifteen rounds. The meeting between the two took place at the Chicago Stadium, Illinois. Robinson found himself a former champion once again when in his second defence he lost a fifteen-round points decision to another American in the shape of Gene Fullmer on 2 January 1957 at Madison Square Garden in New York. Robinson soon got his crown back on 1 May 1957 in a return fight with Fullmer, stopping him in the fifth stanza of a fifteen-round bout. The championship fight took place at the Chicago Stadium, New York. On 23 September 1957, Robinson found himself on the loser's side of a fifteen rounds points decision when defeated in his first defence by fellow countryman Carmen Basilio at the Yankee Stadium in New York. Robinson shocked those who felt his days of being a champion were over when he avenged his former defeat and took back the world middleweight title on 25 March 1958. Sugar Ray outpointed defending champion Carmen Basilio over fifteen rounds. On this occasion, Robinson created a record by regaining the championship on four occasions; this historic event took place at the Chicago Stadium, Illinois.

It was a shock of the highest magnitude when England's Randolph Turpin outpointed defending world middleweight champion Sugar Ray Robinson over fifteen rounds on 10 July 1951 at the Earls Court Arena in Kensington, London. Robinson, who was also a former world welterweight king, entered the ring with an outstanding record of 133 professional bouts with one loss, two draws, and one no contest; he was the overwhelming favourite to win and go back to the States with his crown. Turpin, who by comparison had forty-three paid bouts with one defeat and one draw, was given very little chance at all of victory. Turpin was a good fighter; in fact, he was a very good fighter, but facts are facts—Robinson was exceptional a man who was on course to be a true boxing great. What could Turpin possibly bring to the table to defeat this special champion? To be brutally honest, you would have to say very little. In fact, if Turpin was able to last the full distance with the champion, that indeed would be a feat in itself. Yet on the night, Turpin fought above all expectations to both shock the experts and hence took the title away from Robinson. However, Turpin did not reign for too long for on 12 September 1951, the Englishman met Robinson in a return bout at the Polo Grounds in Manhattan, New York, and surrendered the championship when the American stopped him in round ten of fifteen to regain the title. Robinson got his revenge and his championship back but he could not take away from Turpin that magical night when he became the king of the middleweight division.

Former world heavyweight king Joe Louis bowed out from professional boxing on 26 October 1951 when stopped in the eighth round of a scheduled ten by Rocky Marciano at Madison Square Garden in New York. While Marciano fought well in this contest, it was painfully obvious that this was not the Louis of old. The 'Brown Bomber' as he was nicknamed was past his very best and was not able to execute the moves he once could. Louis left the sport on a losing note but the fighter had ensured with his fine ability during the early years that his name would be enshrined with the greats of the division. Louis won sixty-six and lost three of his professional bouts and holds the record of having made more successful successive defences of the world heavyweight title than any other champion in the division, the total being twenty-five.

On 19 May 1952, Yoshio Shiral became the first Japanese-born fighter to win a world title in the professional ranks. Shiral showed his ring skills, outpointing defending world flyweight champion Dado Marino of Hawaii over the duration of fifteen rounds. The contest took place at the Korakuen Baseball Stadium, Tokyo.

It is not too unusual to see a fighter fail to go the full distance in a world title bout but it is a little unusual when the referee fails to do so. Such an event took place on 25 June 1952 when Sugar Ray Robinson (the former world welterweight king and then-current world middleweight champion) looked set to win his third world title when he stepped into the ring at the Yankee Stadium, New York City, to challenge Joey Maxim for the light-heavyweight crown. Robinson had an impressive professional record of 137 bouts with two defeats, two draws, and one no contest. Maxim too had a fight ledger worthy of respect: seventy-eight wins, eighteen defeats, and four draws. Joey had won the world crown when he knocked out Britain's Freddie Mills in round ten of fifteen on 24 January 1950 at the Earls Court Empress Hall in Kensington, London. The defence against Robinson would be his second, having outpointed challenger and fellow American Bob Murphy over fifteen rounds on 22 August 1951 at Madison Square Garden, Manhattan. While Robinson appeared to have the skill set to defeat Maxim, no one took into consideration the weather conditions on the day and to be fair, why should they? Yet oddly, it would have a strong bearing on the outcome of the fight, which would affect not just the boxer's performance but the referee's also. The heat was excessive, reported to be at that time in the region of 104–107 degrees inside the ring. The referee in charge, Ruby Goldstein, was taken ill during the contest; he was so badly affected by the high temperature that he had to be replaced by Ray Miller after round ten. If it was tough for the referee, it had to be even tougher for the two boxers—a fact that was confirmed when in round fourteen, a completely drained Robinson retired in his corner after taking a clear points lead. Had the elements been normal, Sugar Ray may well have won the championship and Goldstein would most certainly have lasted the full distance of fifteen rounds.

Jimmy Carruthers won the world bantamweight title on 15 November 1952 when he challenged South African title-holder Vic Toweel at the Rand Stadium in Johannesburg, winning in sensational fashion by a knockout in the opening round in a bout set for fifteen. On this occasion, Carruthers became the first Australian-born boxer to win an undisputed world crown and the first fighter with the southpaw stance to capture a title in this division. Carruthers won the Commonwealth championship that Toweel was also defending at the time.

On 26 March 1953, George Walker from London stepped into the ring at The Stadium, Liverpool, to contest the vacant British light-heavyweight crown against Welsh-born opponent Dennis Powell. The pair had met previously on 30 September 1952 at Earls Court, Empress Hall in Kensington, when Powell emerged victorious in the third session by disqualification in a scheduled ten rounder. Experience was on the side of Powell, who had a record of sixty-three fights (winning thirty-nine, losing twenty, and drawing four of his bouts) with Walker having participated in eleven bouts (winning nine with two defeats). The contest was scheduled for the distance of fifteen rounds but did not go that far. The bout was stopped in the eleventh round in favour of Powell. Both men gave the spectators value for money in an action-packed encounter. Upon his eventual requirement from the rigours of the ring, Walker would later manage his younger brother heavyweight Billy Walker. During his career, Billy became a firm favourite with fight fans, hence being the undisputed king of the box office—such was his popularity, there were few empty seats (if any) when Billy fought.

Australian Jimmy Carruthers made the third defence title of his world bantamweight title against home fighter Chamroen Songkitrat at the National Gymnasium Stadium in Bangkok, Thailand, on 2 May 1954. Both men not only had themselves to battle but the elements which made their task that much more difficult resulting in an unusual occurrence. The fight took place in an open-air stadium and the rain poured down during their meeting. Both men hence were forced to fight in their bare feet rather than boots, thus ensuring they did not slip on the wet canvas during their encounter. Despite the difficulties, Carruthers retained the title with a twelve-round points decision.

Future two-time world heavyweight king Floyd Patterson was clearly taking a big leap up in class on 7 June 1954 when he was matched with former world light-heavyweight king Joey Maxim—a good fighter without a doubt, a man who during his career had met the best the ring had to offer. Maxim had an impressive record of 105 bouts (winning eighty, losing twenty-one, and drawing four). Patterson by comparison was undefeated in thirteen bouts. The two battled it out at the Eastern Parkway Arena, Brooklyn. The contest went the full eight rounds with Maxim's experience proving too much for his young opponent, hence Patterson sustained his first loss by way of a points decision.

Rocky Marciano made the sixth and last defence of his world heavyweight title on 21 September 1955 when he dramatically knocked out challenger Archie Moore in round nine of a scheduled fifteen at the Yankee Stadium in New York. Rocky had captured the championship on 23 September 1952 by knocking out defending title-holder Jersey Joe Walcott in round thirteen of fifteen at the Municipal Stadium in Philadelphia. Many fighters over the years have gone on too long, having that one fight too many. So it was refreshing when Rocky came to the

Floyd Patterson suffered his first professional defeat in 1954 against former world light-heavyweight champion Joey Maxim. (*Derek Rowe*)

conclusion that enough was enough and announced his retirement from the ring on 27 April 1956. Marciano had made his last ring appearance at the Yankee Stadium, New York, on 21 September 1955 against challenger Archie Moore. Marciano was the favourite to retain the crown but Moore who was the reigning world light-heavyweight kind looked to be the kind of opponent who could push the champion. Yet once again, Marciano came out on top confirming his position as champion. Rocky left boxing with an unblemished record of forty-nine victories, being the first champion at that time in the division to leave the sport with an undefeated record.

Ray Famechon of France lost the European featherweight title on 3 November 1955 when he stepped into the ring at the Palais des Sports in Paris against challenger Fred Galiana of Spain. Famechon retired in round six of a contest set for fifteen. This proved to be Famechon's last contest for the continental crown; however, he created a record of having participated in more European feather title bouts in the division at that time than any other boxer, the number being thirteen.

During the course of 1956, Derbyshire's Peter Bates locked horns with the Cooper twins (Jim and Henry) and emerged from both encounters with a victory over the Londoners. On 28 February, he met Jim Cooper at the Royal Albert Hall in London in a contest slated for eight rounds. Bates left the ring after scorning a two-round knockout over his opponent. On 7 September, brother Henry (the future British, Commonwealth, and European heavyweight king and world title challenger) stepped into the fray at the King's Hall in Belle Vue, Manchester, to battle Bates in a contest scheduled for ten rounds. Cooper had the extra incentive in this match of gaining revenge for his brother. However, Bates came out on top with a five-round stoppage. It was not until 7 November 1962 that the Cooper family was able to claim a degree of satisfaction. On the night in question, Jim boxed his way to a ten-round points decision over Bates at the Seymour Hall in Marylebone, London.

During his career, Peter Waterman won the British welterweight title when holder Wally Thom retired in round five of a championship bout scheduled for fifteen. The contest took place on 5 June 1956 at the Harringay Area in London. Waterman added to his title collection when he later captured a second championship, winning the European crown at the same venue, stopping Italian Emilio Marconi in round fourteen of fifteen on 28 January 1958. During his career, Waterman defeated and lost to former world welterweight champion Kid Gavilan of Cuba, with both bouts being decided on points after ten rounds. Peter retired from the sport with a record of forty-seven bouts (winning forty-two, drawing two, and losing three). Interestingly, his younger brother Dennis did not follow him into the professional ring but found fame in the acting profession, playing the role of George Carter in *The Sweeney*, later Terry McCann (an ex-boxer) in *Minder*, and Gerry Standing in *New Tricks* plus many other numerous parts on TV and in films.

Hungary's Laszlo Papp fought his way into the history books of amateur boxing at the 1956 Olympic Games, which took place in Melbourne, Australia. Papp outpointed American Jose Torres to win a gold medal at light middleweight. In so doing, Papp became the first fighter to win three consecutive gold medals at the games. The first medal came at middleweight in the 1948 competition in London, outpointing England's Johnny Wright. The second gold was acquired at light-middleweight in the 1952 games at Helsinki, where Papp showed his considerable ring skills to outpoint South African Theunis Jacobus Van Schalkwyk to claim the trinket.

On 30 September 1956, Sweden's Ingemar Johansson won the European heavyweight crown when he knocked out the then champion Franco Cavicchi in round thirteen of a bout set for the duration of fifteen. Even though Cavicchi was defending his title on home turf in front of his home fans at the Stadio Comunale Bologna in Romagna, Italy, he could not get the better of the hard-hitting Swedish challenger. At that moment, Johansson looked a force to be reckoned with on the continent. Strangely, he would go on and become involved in three more European title bouts, all of which would be against fighters from the UK. The first defence took place on 19 May 1957 against Henry Cooper at the Johanneshov Ice Stadium, Stockholm. Cooper was given his 'going home' card when Johansson knocked him out in round five of fifteen. On 21 February 1958, Joe Erskine (the British and Commonwealth champion) was the next to test the power of the Swedish title-holder at the Masshallen, Gothenburg, Sweden. Erskine lasted longer than Cooper, but his bid to win the crown came to an end in round thirteen by way of a stoppage in a bout scheduled for fifteen. After his stint as world heavyweight champion, winning and losing that title to Floyd Patterson, Johansson returned to the European scene to challenge the man who now held his former title: Dick Richardson of Wales, who would be making the fourth defence of the crown against him. The pair met on 17 June 1962 at the Nya Ullevi in Gothenburg, Sweden. Richardson was a hard fighter not to be easily dismissed and would not be intimidated by Johansson's reputation in any way. It did not look for one minute that this contest would go the full fifteen rounds and true enough, it did not; Richardson found himself a former champion when Johansson took him out of the equation by knocking him out in round eight to become champion of Europe for the second time in his career.

Randolph Turpin became the first man to twice regain the British light-heavyweight title when at Granby Halls, Leicester, on 26 November 1956, he stopped former domestic title-holder Alex Buxton in round five for the vacant throne. Turpin first won the championship on 10 June 1952 when he stopped defending champion Don Cockell in round eleven at the White City Stadium in London. On the night, he also won the vacant Commonwealth crown, which was at stake in the bout. Turpin later relinquished the respected titles. Turpin once again turned his attention back to the championship. The reigning champion was Alex Buxton, who was quickly taken out of the fight by Turpin, who knocked him out in round two at the Harringay Arena in London on 26 April 1955. Once again, Turpin relinquished the title. In each case, the title bouts were scheduled for the duration of fifteen rounds.

On 30 November 1956, Floyd Patterson stepped into the square ring with reigning world light-heavyweight champion Archie Moore in a contest scheduled for fifteen rounds to settle the world heavyweight title situation. The former champion Rocky Marciano had retired and a new king had to be crowned. At the Chicago Stadium, Illinois, the vacancy was filled when Patterson landed the decisive blow in round five to claim the championship. In doing so, Patterson scored a double first by becoming (at the age of twenty-one years, ten months, and twenty-six days), the youngest fighter to win the title. It did not stop there; Floyd also became the first Olympic gold medal winner to take this crown. Patterson won gold at middleweight at the games that took place in 1952 in Helsinki, Finland.

American Pete Rademacher won the gold medal at heavyweight in the 1956 Olympic Games, which were held in Melbourne, Australia, by defeating Lev Mukhin of Russia by a knockout in round one. This was of course a magnificent feat—one which often bodes well for the fighter when he turns to the professional ranks. It looked as if Rademacher would, after he joined the 'punch for pay' ranks, work his way up to an eventual crack at the world crown. It was expected that Rademacher would of course indulge in a number of bouts before such a title crack was forthcoming gaining valuable experience before facing the big guns especially a reigning world champion. This is the normal and expected practice in the sport. However, it came as something of a shock when it was announced that his first fight would in fact be a world title challenge. This was a big ask for Rademacher—an assignment where the odds were very much stacked against him. The champion in question at the time was Floyd Patterson, a very experienced fighter. Win or lose, Rademacher was going to make history since he was the first man to challenge for the world heavyweight title in his professional debut. On 22 August 1957, Rademacher stepped into the ring to contest the fifteen-round world championship with Patterson at Sick's Stadium in Seattle. It would have been a sensational victory had Rademacher fought his way to the crown, but it was not to be; it truly was mission impossible and Patterson retained the crown by knockout in round six.

In boxing, one should always expect the unexpected. At the Town Hall in Shoreditch, London, on 14 May 1957, the unexpected happened once again. Briton Terry Downes was signed to meet Nigeria's Dick Tiger in a bout set for eight rounds; the indications suggested he would punch his way to victory, possibly before the final bell had sounded. Terry was the man who looked to have a golden future ahead of him—a fighter on the way to the top. His opposition had other ideas. A tiger in the jungle can be a dangerous proposition and should not be confronted; the Tiger facing Downes in the ring also proved to be a dangerous proposition. Tiger shocked audiences when he stopped Downes in five rounds. On the showing against Downes, Tiger looked to have the potential to make big waves in the sport. However, the spectators who witnessed the bout had no way of knowing that they were actually watching two future world champions in action. In the fullness of time, Tiger won the undisputed world middleweight and light-heavyweight crowns and Downes the NY and EBU version of the middleweight title.

Hogan Kid Bassey became the first fighter from Nigeria to win the world featherweight crown. This event took place on 24 June 1957. Bassey had it all

From left to right: Bobby Neill, Howard Winstone, Walter McGowan, Frankie Taylor, and Terry Downes, who was beaten by Dick Tiger in their meeting in 1957. (*Derek Rowe*)

to do since he was taking on opponent Cherif Hamia on his home ground at the Palais des Sports in Paris, France, for the vacant crown. Cherif would not be beaten easily, but Bassey was not lacking in ring skills and brought them all to bear in the fifteen-round encounter, stopping his man in the tenth round.

On 28 January 1958, Don Jordan went to a ten-round points decision when facing reigning British lightweight champion Dave Charnley at the Harringay Arena in London. Many may now have written off the American when it came to him being a world title-holder; however, in boxing, you never really know. Jordan bounced back from this setback when on 5 December in the same year, he challenged fellow American Virgil Akins for the world welterweight crown at the Olympic Auditorium in Los Angeles, California, and secured the championship with a fifteen-round points decision. This in turn put more value on Charnley's victory over the American.

It looked as if the reign of world light-heavyweight king Archie Moore was fast drawing to a dramatic end in his seventh defence of the title on 10 December 1958 at The Forum in Montreal. Challenger Yvon Durelle made a most promising start to his assault on the championship when he landed his heavy punches, flooring the defending American title-holder three times in the opening session and once more in the fifth. The odds on this bout going the full fifteen rounds looked very remote. So it proved with Moore refusing to yield and showing a champion's heart to fight back and dash Canada's hopes of a new title-holder, knocking out Durelle in round eleven of fifteen.

It was a case of audiences not thinking it would happen when in sensational form, Sweden's Ingemar Johansson ripped the world heavyweight crown from the head of American Floyd Patterson at the Yankee Stadium in New York on 26 June 1959. Patterson, who had previously defended the title successfully on four occasions looked to be the obvious victor when the fight was made. Johansson was good but no one felt that he was good enough to lift the title. The American hold on the title was such that it appeared that any challenger from outside the USA was frankly in the ring just to make up the number. When calling it, you would have to say that Patterson would enter the ring as champion and leave it again as champion when the fight was over. However, Johansson showed that it was foolhardy to write him off without a chance. Johansson turned out to be a dangerous man, more dangerous than those in the know first thought. The referee stepped in to stop what could only be called one-way traffic in the third round of fifteen to save Patterson. This result sent shock waves through boxing. Johansson became the first fighter from Europe to hold this championship since Italy's Primo Carnera who reigned from 1933 to 1934. At that moment in time, only three other non-American fighters had previously held this championship: Bob Fitzsimmons (England, 1897–1899), Tommy Burns (Canada, 1906–1908), and Max Schmeling (Germany, 1930–1932).

5

Round Five: 1960–1969

Pone Kingpetch excelled when he gave Thailand its first-ever professional world boxing champion on 16 April 1960, outpointing defending flyweight title-holder Pascual Perez of Argentina over fifteen rounds. The contest took place at the Lumpinee Boxing Stadium in Bangkok.

On 9 May 1960, Welshman Brian Curvis emulated his older brother Cliff when at the Vetch Field in Swansea, he outpointed holder George Barnes of Australia for the Commonwealth welterweight crown with a fifteen-round points decision. Curvis then further emulated his sibling when, on 21 November 1960, he added the British welterweight title to his name when outpointing Nottingham's reigning champion Wally Swift over the duration of fifteen rounds. The contest that also involved Curvis's Commonwealth crown was staged at the Ice Rink in Nottingham. Brian's brother, Cliff Curvis, had won the British and Commonwealth crowns in the division on 24 July 1952 at the Stadium in Liverpool, knocking out Merseyside's defending champion Wally Thom in round nine in a bout slated for fifteen.

Rene Libeer of France tried his hand on three occasions in attempting to gain a victory in the UK. Libeer first attempt took place on 31 May 1960 against Northern Ireland's Johnny Caldwell at the Empire Pool in Wembley, London, losing a ten-round points decision. The Frenchman was in action once again on 5 June 1962 against another fighter from Northern Ireland: Freddie Gilroy, the reigning British and Commonwealth and former European bantamweight champion. The battle that took place at the Empire Pool in Wembley, London, saw Libeer finish second when Giroy was awarded the decision on points after ten rounds. On 16 October, the venue again being the Empire Pool, Libeer faced Walter

McGowan from Scotland and due to a cut eye, he was stopped in the sixth session of scheduled ten. To his credit, when stepping into British rings, Libeer was meeting quality fighters and not easy touches. Despite these defeats, Libeer continued his trade and on 13 June 1965, he contested the vacant European flyweight title against Paul Chervet of Switzerland at the Salle Roger Salengro in Wattrelos, France. In the fifteenth and final round, the contest was stopped in Libeer's favour, seeing him become the new champion and the first French holder of the title in this division since Louis Skena who reigned from 1953–54.

No fighter had ever regained the world heavyweight title until American Floyd Patterson who on 20 June 1960 became the first to do so at the Polo Grounds in Manhattan. Patterson dethroned Sweden's Ingemar Johansson by a five-round knockout in a bout scheduled for fifteen to wear the crown once more. In their previous encounter on 26 June 1959, Johansson had taken the title from Patterson by way of a three-round stoppage at the Yankee Stadium in the Bronx, New York. In their second battle, Patterson more than redeemed himself. A third meeting between the two had to happen; a final decider was precisely what the fans wanted to see. Patterson and Johansson entered the ring to renew hostilities on 13 March 1961 at the Convention Center in Miami Beach, Florida. The contest was not expected to go the full fifteen-round course and this expectation was proven correct when Patterson confirmed his superiority by knocking out Johansson in round six to retain the title.

The then reigning British and Commonwealth light-heavyweight king Chic Calderwood outpointed American Willie Pastrano on 16 September 1960 at the Kelvin Hall in Glasgow, Scotland. This proved to be the Scot's best win in the professional ranks since Pastrano later won the undisputed world title at light-heavyweight. The event took place at the Convention Center in Nevada, Las Vegas, when on 1 June 1963, Pastrano outpointed fellow countryman Harold Johnson over fifteen rounds to take the crown.

On 27 September 1960, Terry Spinks captured the British featherweight crown by stopping defending champion Scotland's Bobby Neill in round seven of a scheduled fifteen. The contest which took place at the Royal Albert Hall in Kensington, London, was one of historic significance for Londoner Spinks was the first UK Olympic gold medallist to win a British title in the professional ranks. Terry had won gold at flyweight in the Olympic Games, which took place in Melbourne, Australia, during 1956.

During his career, Japan's Mitsunori Seki attempted on five occasions to capture a world title. Seki's first attempt took place on 27 June 1961 at the Kokugikan Arena in Tokyo against defending world flyweight king Pone Kingpetch from Thailand. After fifteen rounds of boxing, Kingpetch was given the decision and kept his crown. On 1 March 1964, Seki stepped in with Cuban-born but Mexican-resident Sugar Ramos in his attempt to win the world featherweight crown; again, Seki was given home ground advantage, the venue being the Kokugikan Arena in Tokyo. The fans got behind Seki and gave him their support and encouragement; however, it was to no avail. Ramos retained his title when Seki retired in round six of fifteen. Seki once again attempted to take the world featherweight championship but this time, he had to travel to Mexico to meet the then reigning title-holder Vicente Saldivar at the El Toredo de Cuatro Camino in Mexico City. On 7 August 1966, Saldivar delighted his home fans when he outpointed his Japanese challenger over fifteen rounds to retain the title. Seki returned to Mexico once again on 29 January 1967 in another bid to take the world featherweight crown. Seki hence challenged Saldivar at the same venue the El Toredo de Cuatro. Try as he might, Seki was unable to fight his way to victory and the championship he so desired when he was stopped in round seven of a scheduled fifteen. At this time, it appeared that there would be no more chances for Seki to win a world title. Such an assumption was proven wrong following the unexpected retirement of Saldivar the championship door was wide open once again for Seki and he was given the opportunity to contest the vacant WBC world featherweight title. At the Royal Albert Hall in London, Seki confronted Howard Winstone on 23 January 1968 for the crown he hoped he would take back to Japan. There would be no fairy tale ending for Seki for once again, he suffered defeat when he was stopped in round nine of fifteen in what proved to be his last professional bout.

Jim Cooper travelled to the Kelvin Hall in Glasgow, Scotland, on 9 August 1961 to do battle. The Londoner looked to have a tough night ahead of him, being matched with the British and Commonwealth light-heavyweight king Chic Calderwood in a non-title bout. When viewing all aspects of the meeting between the two, a win for Calderwood was the expected result. However, at the end of the contest that went the full ten rounds, a mild surprise took place when a drawn decision was rendered. Cooper was the twin brother of the then British and Commonwealth heavyweight king Henry Cooper.

In just his third professional contest, Walter McGowan attempted to increase his undefeated record and also add the Scottish flyweight title to his name when he challenged the reigning champion Jackie Brown. Brown was making the first defence of the crown and was entering the ring with a slate of twenty fights (winning sixteen with three defeats and one no contest). On the night of 25 October 1961, Brown retained the title with an eight-round points victory at the Ice Rink in Paisley, Scotland. The pair met once again at the same venue on 2 May 1963. Brown was now the British and Commonwealth flyweight king and would be putting these titles on the line against McGowan in his first defence. Brown now had a résumé of twenty-seven fights with twenty-two wins and four defeats with one no contest while McGowan had a record of nine bouts with just that one defeat, hence the champion still had the edge in experience over his challenger. That said, experience meant nothing on the night when McGowan seized his opportunity and gained revenge for his previous defeat, knocking out Brown in the twelfth session of a fifteen-round scheduled contest.

In defence of his British, European, and Commonwealth lightweight titles (which took place on 20 November 1961), Dave Charnley clearly had no intention of travelling the full fifteen rounds. In fact, he had a very early night when he knocked out challenger Darkie Hughes in the first round at the Ice Rink in Nottingham. In so doing, he produced at the time the fastest win in a British championship contest with the bout lasting just forty seconds.

On 27 March 1962, Billy Walker (the former 1961 ABA heavyweight champion) made his professional debut at the Empire Pool in Wembley, London, stopping Belgium's Jose Peyre in round five of eight. This was the start of an exciting ride in the heavyweight division for the promising London-born boxer. While you will not see the name of Walker on any official lists of champions, there was no doubt that he was the undisputed box-office champion in the UK; whenever he fought, the fans would flock to see him in action. Billy always gave everything, win or lose when in the ring.

Billy did make two attempts at winning a title. He failed on 21 March 1967 when Germany's Karl Mildenberger stopped him in round eight in a scheduled fifteen when defending the European crown at the Empire Pool, Wembley. Once again at the same venue, on 7 November 1967, Billy drew a blank when he was stopped by holder Henry Cooper in round six in a contest scheduled for fifteen when challenging for the British and Commonwealth heavyweight titles. Walker's career ended where it started at the Empire Pool, Wembley, when stopped in round eight of a ten-round contest by Jack Bodell. During his career, Walker fought on thirty-one occasions (winning twenty-one, losing eight, and drawing two of his bouts).

It was a special night for the domestic featherweight division on 30 May 1962; for the first time, two Welsh boxers were going to contest the British featherweight title. Howard Winstone was making the second defence of his domestic crown at the Maindy Stadium in Cardiff against Harry Carroll. Winstone first won the title from holder Terry Spinks from London on 2 May 1961 at the Empire Pool, putting in a stylish performance to stop him in round ten of a fifteen-round contest. The first

From left to right: Reg Gutteridge (boxing journalist and TV commentator), Walter McGowan (who in 1963 defeated fellow Scot Jackie Brown for the British and Commonwealth flyweight titles), and Eamonn Andrews (radio and TV presenter). (*Derek Rowe*)

Exciting heavyweight Billy Walker (right) became a box-office magnet in the UK; here he is attacking his opponent, who is forced onto the ropes. (*Derek Rowe*)

defence by the Welshman was made against Scotland's Derry Treanor on 10 April 1962 once again at the Empire Pool. Treanor pushed Winstone hard in his attempt to take the crown and it looked as if he would take the dual into the fifteenth and final round, but the champion proved to be the boss and retained his crown by stopping the fighting Scot in the fourteenth session. In his bout with Carroll, Winstone retained the title once again when his challenger retired in round six of fifteen.

Israel saw its first-ever professional boxing contest on 26 June 1962 when former two-time world bantamweight king Alphonse Halimi of France challenged Italy's reigning European bantamweight title-holder Piero Rollo at the Basa Stadium, Tel Aviv. The contest went the full duration of fifteen rounds with Halimi becoming the new champion when receiving the points decision.

Chic Calderwood put on the gloves to contest the vacant European light-heavyweight title on 28 September 1962 at the Palazzetto dello Sport in Rome, Italy. Calderwood was up against a worthy opponent in Giulio Rinaldi, who had the advantage of fighting in front of his home fans so the

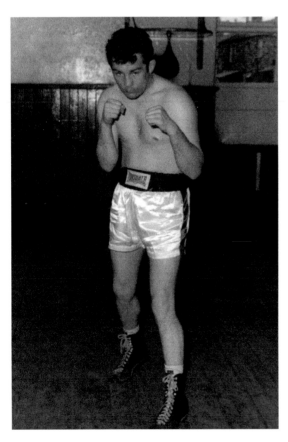

Howard Winstone defeated Harry Carroll to win a Lonsdale Belt outright.
(*Derek Rowe*)

task in front of the Briton was a tough one. Calderwood had been the first Scottish boxer to win the British title at the poundage on 28 January 1960 when he won the vacant crown stopping England's Arthur Howard in round thirteen of fifteen at the Ice Rink in Paisley, Scotland. Calderwood next added to his title collection by stopping Tonga's Johnny Halafihi in round twelve for the vacant Commonwealth crown in a contest scheduled for fifteen. The contest took place at Firhill Park in Glasgow, Scotland, on 9 June 1960. Calderwood was however unable to make it a trio of firsts when Rinaldi outpointed Calderwood over fifteen rounds to take the continental crown.

In the inaugural contest for the WBA world super-welterweight title, which took place on 20 October 1962, Denny Moyer stepped into the ring to face fellow American Joey Giambra at the Memorial Coliseum in Portland, Oregon. After fifteen rounds, Moyer was awarded the decision on points, to be crowned the first-ever champion at the weight. Interestingly, the referee of the contest was the then reigning world heavyweight champion Sonny Liston. Prior to the Moyer–Giambra encounter, a contest took place on 17 October 1962 that pitted Emile Griffith against American Ted Wright at the Stadthalle in Vienna, Austria. Griffith, who was born in the Virgin Islands, won a fifteen-round points decision and was given recognition by the Austrian Boxing Board of Control as being the new super-welterweight champion. In truth, this claim was not taken seriously and the Moyer–Giambra bout is generally regarded as being the first world championship to be staged in the division.

During their professional careers, Dick Tiger of Nigeria and American Gene Fullmer fought in three consecutive world middleweight title bouts. On 23 October 1962, Tiger defeated Fullmer by a fifteen-round points decision to win the vacant WBA world middleweight crown at Candlestick Park in San Francisco. In a return that took place on 23 February 1963 at the Convention Centre in Las Vegas, Tiger retained the WBA title by a draw over fifteen rounds. In a third and final clash, which took place at the Liberty Stadium in Ibadan, Nigeria, on 10 August 1963, Tiger proved his supremacy when Fullmer retired in round seven of fifteen in a bout for the then undisputed championship. This was the first world middleweight championship to be staged in Nigeria.

On 28 October 1962, Italy's Piero Rollo challenged former two-time world bantamweight champion Alphonse Halimi of France for the European bantamweight crown at the Stadio Amsicora Cagliari Sardegna in Italy. Rollo had previously lost this title to Halimi on 26 June 1962 by a fifteen-round points decision at the Basa Stadium in Tel Aviv. Rollo hence gained revenge in their second meeting by regaining the crown when earning a fifteen-round points decision. By doing so, Rollo became the first fighter in this division to win the title on three separate occasions. Rollo first won the championship on 12 October 1958 when he met the then title-holder Mario D'Agata also of Italy at the Stadio Amsicora, Cagliari Sardegna. Rollo lost the crown to Ireland's reigning British and Commonwealth king Freddie Gilroy in his third defence on points over fifteen rounds at the Empire Pool on 3 November 1959. Rollo failed in his attempt to regain the championship on 4 November 1961 when Pierre Cossemyns of Belgium, the then title-holder, won a fifteen-round points verdict in Cagliari, Italy. In a return that took place in Brussels, Belgium, on 13 April 1962, Rollo took back the title when knocking out Cossemyns in round five of a scheduled fifteen-round encounter to wear the crown for a second time. Rollo's professional career drew to an end on 12 March 1964 whereupon he outpointed his Spanish opponent Rafael Fernandez over ten rounds in Genoa, Italy. The former three-time European title-holder's career set a record of eighty-one bouts (winning sixty-one, losing thirteen, and drawing seven).

It is often said that 'three's a charm' and so it proved on 25 February 1963 at the King's Hall in Belle Vue, Manchester. British lightweight champion Dave Charnley stopped former world lightweight king Joe Brown in round six in a contest set for ten. This was their third meeting inside the ring and the first occasion for Charnley to score a victory over his American opponent. On 2 December 1959, Charnley met Brown for the first time at the Sam Houston Coliseum in Houston whereupon the Briton was stopped in round six of fifteen due to a cut over his right eye in his challenge for the world lightweight crown. In a return on 18 April 1961 at Earls Court Arena in Kensington, London, hopes were running high that a British victory would be achieved; it would not be easy but Charnley had the class to take the win. It was, however, disappointment once again when the fifteen rounds points decision went to the American thus seeing him retain the title. When the Briton eventually defeated Brown, he no longer held the world title. At least Charnley did get a degree of satisfaction by at long last gaining a victory over his opponent.

Future undisputed world welterweight champion Curtis Cokes of America looked impressive in his twelve-round bout against opponent and countryman Flory Olguin on 30 May 1963. The battle between the two fighters took place at the Civic Auditorium in Albuquerque, New Mexico, and concluded when Cokes stopped his opponent in round five. The referee in charge of the contest was an imposing figure in the shape of the then reigning undisputed world heavyweight champion Sonny Liston.

After a period of fifteen years, three months, and seventeen days, the European featherweight title finally returned to UK shores courtesy of Howard Winstone, the reigning British champion. Welsh-born Winstone put on a fine exhibition of boxing at the Maindy Stadium in Cardiff on 9 July 1963 to take the crown from Italy's defending champion Alberto Serti who was halted in round fourteen of the fifteen round scheduled contest. The last British holder of this crown prior to Winstone was Blackpool's Ronnie Clayton, who lost the title when Frenchman Ray Famechon outpointed him over fifteen rounds to claim the crown on 22 March 1948, the venue being the Ice Rink, Nottingham.

On 9 December 1963, Risto Luukkonen became the first boxer from Finland to win a European title in two different weight divisions when he outscored defending European bantamweight king Mimoun Ben Ali of Spain over fifteen rounds. This bout took place in Helsinki, Finland. Luukkonen won his first European crown at the flyweight poundage on 4 September 1959 when he defeated another Spaniard, Young Martin, the reigning champion by a fifteen-round points decision once again in Helsinki. Luukkonen became an ex-flyweight champion when in his first defence on 29 June 1961, he lost a fifteen-round points decision to Italian Salvatore Burruni (a future world flyweight king in a contest, which took place in Alghero, Sardegna in Italy).

Olli Maki of Finland outpointed opponent Conny Rudhof of Germany in Helsinki over fifteen rounds to emerge as the first-ever holder of the European super-lightweight championship. The contest took place on 14 February 1964. Going into the contest, Maki had racked up sixteen fights (winning twelve, losing two, and drawing two) with his opponent Rudhof having had fifty-five bouts (winning forty-eight, losing four, and drawing two with one no contest).

Going into the contest, reigning British and Commonwealth flyweight king Walter McGowan had amassed a record of thirteen fights (winning twelve and losing one); he looked to be in for a tough night on 4 March 1964. McGowan was to face the reigning European bantamweight king Risto Luukkonen of Finland in a ten round non-title contest. Luukkonen had fought on thirty-five occasions (winning twenty-nine, losing four, and drawing two). McGowan was an undoubted talent, but was the man from Finland one step too far? Would Luukkonen know too much for him? At the Ice Rink in Paisley, McGowan answered those two poignant questions when he scored an excellent victory on points. This was clearly McGowan's best win at that particular time in the professional ranks, one which would boost his stock considerably in the European and world rankings.

The first contest for the European super-welterweight championship took place on 22 May 1964. Bruno Visintin of Italy and Yoland Leveque of France squared up to contest the inaugural title at the Palazzo dello Sport in Torino, Italy. The two fighters battled for the full fifteen rounds and at the final bell, Visintin was crowned the king of Europe at the weight.

Vicente Saldivar of Mexico and Panama's Ismael Laguna engaged in a ten-round contest at the Plazza de Toros Baja in Tijuana, Mexico, on 1 June 1964. Saldivar emerged the victor when winning a points decision. Both boxers were remarkable exponents of their trade and showed their skills in this meeting. It was not surprising that both fighters would go on and eventually win a world championship. Laguna twice won the undisputed lightweight title. Saldivar twice won the world featherweight crown first the undisputed crown then later the WBC version of the title.

Laszlo Papp of Hungary made a sixth successful defence of his European middleweight crown on 9 October 1964 when he outpointed British middleweight king Mick Leahy of Ireland over fifteen rounds at the Stadthalle in Vienna, Austria. With a record of forty-six victories with fifteen defeats and seven draws, Leahy fought his best but was always one step behind the champion who had a résumé of twenty-six wins with two draws. At that moment, Papp was an outstanding amateur boxer (a fact backed by his winning of three gold medals at the Olympics); he looked on the verge of challenging for the world championship. The holder of the title was Joey Giardello of America and while the champion was obviously a worthy adversary for Papp it was not beyond the realms of impossibility that the Hungarian would have taken the title had they met. At that time, professional boxing was not allowed in Hungary but Papp was allowed to fight in that code. However, the Hungarian Government later decided to revoke Papp's permit to travel, which sadly brought an end to his career.

There is no argument that American Sugar Ray Robinson is one of the unchallenged greats in the sport of boxing. Robinson is a fighter who won both the World welterweight and middleweight world titles during his long career inside the square ring. Robinson had splendid skills and was a joy to watch when in action. Yet it is amazing that this outstanding boxer who made four visits to the UK could only gain victory in one contest. That win came about on 12 October 1964 against Johnny Angel at the Hilton Hotel in Mayfair, London, by a six-round stoppage in a bout scheduled for eight. This was not vintage Robinson—not the man who had once exchanged punches with the best in both the welterweight and middleweight divisions. It was obvious that his prime was now behind him, lost in the shadows of time, but he still had some of the moves that once took him to the top in both the two weight divisions. Robinson first paid a visit to British shores on 10 July 1951 when defending his world middleweight crown against homegrown Randolph Turpin at the Earls Court Arena in Kensington, London. Turpin was on top of his game and surged to a fifteen-round points decision to nab the title. It was one of the biggest shocks in boxing at the time. Some years later, Sugar Ray returned to mix it up with former world and British middleweight king Terry Downes at the Empire Pool in Wembley, London, on 25 September 1962. Sugar did not find the occasion very sweet went he went down to a ten-round points decision to Downes. Then on 3 September 1964, Robinson found himself facing reigning British middleweight champion Mick Leahy. The venue for the contest between Leahy and Robinson was the Ice Rink in Paisley, Scotland. Things did not go the former two weight world champion's way. When the bell sounded to end the ten-round contest, Leahy's hand was raised in victory.

On 30 November 1964, American Willie Pastrano retained his world light-heavyweight crown at the Kings Hall, Belle Vue, Manchester, when he stopped former New York and European world and British middleweight champion Terry Downes in round eleven of fifteen. Pastrano was, prior to this contest, a regular visitor to UK shores with mixed fortunes. Pastrano made his first appearance in the UK on 22 October 1957, outpointing Dick Richardson over ten rounds at the Harringay Arena in London. At the same venue on 25 February 1958, Pastrano scored another victory when he outpointed Brian London over ten rounds. Willie boxed his way to another win when he outpointed Jamaican Joe Bygraves over ten rounds at the Granby Halls in Leicester on 21 April 1958. The tide turned against Pastrano when in a return bout with Brian London on 30 September 1958 at the Harringay Arena when he was stopped in round five of ten. Then in his next visit, Joe Erskine outpointed Pastrano over ten rounds on 24 February 1959 at Wembley Stadium in London. On 16 September 1960, Chic Calderwood outpointed Pastrano over the duration of ten rounds at the Kelvin Hall in Glasgow, Scotland.

When it came to winning European title fights, Italy was not always the most successful hunting ground for UK fighters. Welshman Howard Winstone proved to be the exception to the rule. On 22 January 1965, he put his European featherweight crown on the line against French challenger Yves Desmarets at the Palazzetto dello Sport in Rome and retained his crown with a fifteen-round points decision. In his next defence of the title, he once again ventured to Italy, this time the venue being the Teatro Verdi in Sassari, Sardegna, against Andrea Silanos in a bout that took place on 7 March 1966. This time around, the assignment looked a little riskier for Winstone since Silanos was an Italian fighting in front of his home supporters. The defence against Desmarets was a neutral affair with one fighter of course being French the other British. If there were any concerns for Winstone in this encounter they were proven to be unfounded since the Welsh wizard stopped his challenger in the fifteenth and final round to ensure that he was going home still the champion of Europe.

During their careers, Carlos Ortiz of Purto Rico and Ismael Laguna of Panama squared off in three world lightweight titles bouts and oddly enough on two occasions, the third man in charge of the proceedings in the ring was a former world heavyweight champion. On 10 April 1965, Ortiz lost his lightweight crown when dropping a fifteen-round points decision to Laguna in a contest that took place at the Estadio Nacional, Panama. The referee on that occasion was Jersey Joe Walcott. A return between the two on 13 November 1965 at the Hiram Bithorn Stadium in San Juan, Puerto Rico, saw Ortiz take back the world championship with a fifteen-round points decision. The referee of this bout was Rocky Marciano.

American Ronnie Jones had a degree of success when plying his trade in the UK. Jones first engagement in Britain took place in Scotland at the Ice Rink in Paisley against former British and Commonwealth flyweight king Jackie Brown on 10 June 1965. The contest was set for ten rounds but did not go that far when Brown was knocked out in round two. The second appearance by Jones once again saw him in the rink at the Ice Rink on 20 August 1965. The reigning British and Commonwealth flyweight king Walter McGowan was in the opposite corner. When the bell sounded, McGowan quickly showed his class, outboxing his American foe and looking well on his way to certain victory as the rounds passed by. Once again, Jones scored a victory when a badly cut right eye sustained by McGowan saw the contest curtailed in round six of ten. However, the third outing in the UK for Jones took place at the Royal Albert Hall in Kensington, London, on 12 December 1967 where he would go toe to toe with former British and Commonwealth bantamweight champion Alan Rudkin. It had to be wondered if the American would make it a trio of wins on the night. However, Rudkin in fine form became the terminator when he found the punch to knock out the American in round two of a scheduled ten.

Argentina's Eduardo Corletti fought in a British ring on six occasions during his professional career, winning five and losing one of his bouts. Corletti's first outing in the UK took place on 19 October 1965 at the Empire Pool, where he stopped home fighter Billy Walker in round eight of ten. The pair previously boxed a ten-round draw at the Teatro Ariston in Sanremo, Italy. Corletti's second outing took place on 25 January 1966 at the Olympia, Kensington, London, outpointing Canada's rugged George Chuvalo over ten rounds. Next up was Jamaican-born former Commonwealth heavyweight champion Joe Bygraves, who like Chuvalo suffered a ten-round points decision defeat on 20 March 1967. The pair fought at the Hilton Hotel in Mayfair, London. South African Gerry de Bruyn was another who (at the end of a ten-round contest at the Kings Hall, Belle Vue, Manchester, on 15 May 1967) saw Corletti's arm raised in victory. Britain's Johnny Prescott was unable to stem the tide of the visitor from Argentina when on 17 October 1967, he too tasted defeat when going down to a ten-round points defeat at the Royal Albert Hall in Kensington, London. All things come to an end and so did Corletti's winning streak in the UK when on 6 October 1970 when at the Royal Albert Hall, he was outpointed by future British, European, and Commonwealth heavyweight champion Joe Bugner over ten rounds.

While winning the British, European, and Commonwealth bantamweight titles during his career, it appeared that Alan Rudkin was not fated to add the world crown to his collection. In three attempts that saw him venture abroad, Rudkin came up empty. On 30 November 1965, the Briton challenged Fighting Harada at the Nippon Budokan in Tokyo; after giving his all, Rudkin lost a fifteen-round points decision. The next crack at the crown saw Rudkin travel down under to meet Lionel Rose at the Kooyong Tennis Stadium in Melbourne, Australia, on 8 March 1969. Rose had taken the championship from Harara on 27 February 1968, securing the victory with a fifteen-round points decision. Rudkin undoubtedly had a difficult night's work ahead of him against an accomplished fighter defending on home ground. At the end of the fifteen-round encounter with Rudkin, Rose retained his crown with a fifteen-round points victory and also won the Briton's Commonwealth title which was also on the line. A third opportunity to win the crown took place on 12 December 1969

Argentina's Eduardo Corletti (left) found the UK a most successful country to show his skills. (*Derek Rowe*)

when Rudkin met Mexico's Ruben Olivares at the Forum Inglewood in Los Angeles. Olivares had ripped the championship from Rose with a devastating display of power, stopping the Australian in five rounds of fifteen on 22 August 1969. Few if any gave Rudkin a chance of bringing the prized title home or even going the full route of fifteen rounds and their pessimism proved correct when the challenger was stopped in the second session.

On 3 December 1965, it looked as if British and Commonwealth flyweight king Walter McGowan was going to be the first boxer from the UK to win a European bantamweight crown on Italian territory when he challenged home fighter Tommaso Galli for the crown. McGowan had moved up a division to challenge for the title. The contest was staged at the Palazetto dello Sport, Roma in Lazio, Italy, in a bout set for the duration of fifteen rounds. McGowan boxed in a masterful way, suggesting that he

Alan Rudkin tried on three occasions to win the world bantamweight title but came up against exceptional champions and hence failed each time. (*Derek Rowe*)

would emerge the new champion when the points were totted up at the end of the contest, which went the full route of fifteen rounds. Sadly for the talented Scot and British boxing, it was a case of close but no cigar when the bout was declared a draw, which of course meant that Galli remained king of the continent.

Jack London Jr entered the ring at the Tower Circus in Blackpool, Lancashire on 1 February 1966 in a return bout with Lloyd Walford. The two light-heavyweights had fought before at the City Hall in Sheffield, Yorkshire, on 18 November 1965. On that occasion, Walford left the ring with a stoppage victory in the eighth and final round over his opponent. London Jr was looking for revenge over Walford, who had a record of seven wins with nine defeats and one draw. However, Walford scored the double when he once again stopped his man this time in the third of an eight-round clash. This proved to be London Jr's last excursion into the ring retiring with a professional record of thirty wins with thirteen defeats two draws and one no contest. Boxing clearly run through the veins of the London family with father Jack London holding the British and Commonwealth heavyweight crown from 1944–1945 and younger brother Brian following suit also holding the British and Commonwealth heavyweight titles from 1958–1959.

The first world heavyweight title bout to be staged in the UK for over fifteen years, eleven months, and fifteen days took place on 21 May 1966 at the Arsenal Football Ground in Highbury, London, between defending champion Muhammad Ali and British challenger Henry Cooper. Cooper was always dangerous with his left hook known as 'Enry's Ammer'—a damaging blow if it landed on target, a fact many opponents of the Londoner would testify to. Ali was more than aware of the damage Cooper could do with his renowned punch if it landed square on his chin. Ali (then called Cassius Clay) came to the UK on 18 June 1963 to engage Cooper in a ten-round contest at Wembley Stadium, and found himself dumped on his backside in round four when caught by the Londoner's left hook, which often said goodnight to his opponents. Ali beat the count and went on to stop Cooper in the next round on cuts. Ali was cautious in their second meeting and was able to evade Cooper's fight-ending blow and hence retained his WBC title when he stopped Cooper in round six of a scheduled fifteen due to a badly cut left eye. The last world heavyweight bout to take place in Britain was between Lee Savold of the USA and British Bruce Woodcock at the White City Stadium on 6 June 1950. The prize on offer at that time was the vacant British and European version of the championship. Savold won the title on that occasion when Woodcock thus retired in round four of their respective bout, which was set for fifteen.

On 14 June 1966, Walter McGowan challenged Italy's Salvatore Burruni for the Lineal EBU and British world flyweight crown (prior to this meeting,

Muhammad Ali turned back the challenge of Henry Cooper for the WBC world heavyweight crown in 1966. (*Derek Rowe*)

Burruni had been stripped of the WBC and WBA versions of the crown) at the Empire Pool, London. The pair had previously met when on 24 April 1964, the Scot ventured to the Stadio Olimpico in Rome, Italy, to challenge the Italian for the European flyweight crown and returned home empty-handed after losing a fifteen-round points decision. This time, McGowan was more experienced and his ring skills had improved greatly since their first meeting. The tables were turned on Burruni when McGowan put in a fine performance to outpoint the defending title-holder over the duration of fifteen rounds to take the championship. McGowan became the first fighter from the UK to win a world championship in this division since England's Terry Allen, who won and lost the crown in 1950.

Italy's Nino Benvenuti stepped into the ring at Changchung Gymnasium in Seoul, South Korea, on 25 June 1966 to defend his WBA world super-welterweight title against Ki-Soo Kim. Despite fighting in the challenger's back yard, it looked a safe defence for the talented champion. The signs were that Benvenuti would at the end of the proceedings go home with his title safely packed away in his case. However, Ki-Soo Kim sprung a surprise and claimed a fifteen-round points decision to take the crown and hence Benvenuti's undefeated record, which had stood at an unblemished sixty-five prior to this contest. In so doing, Kim became his country's first world champion.

From left to right: Howard Winstone, Alan Rudkin, and Walter McGowan, who won the lineal version of the world flyweight crown in 1966 by defeating Italy's Salvatore Burruni. (*Derek Rowe*)

Muhammad Ali was the first world heavyweight champion to defend his title against challengers who fought in the southpaw stance. The first occasion took place on 10 September 1966 against the reigning European champion Karl Mildenberger of Germany. The contest took place at the Waldstadion/ Radrennbahn, Frankfurt. Ali emerged successful when he retained his WBC crown by stopping his brave challenger in round twelve in a contest set for the duration of fifteen. The second southpaw to attempt to win the title was Richard Dunn from the UK who at the time held the British, European, and Commonwealth crowns. Once again, the world championship took place in Germany, the venue being the Olympiahalle in Munich. Ali once again proved supreme in this meeting on 24 May 1976, stopping Dunn in round five of fifteen, thus retaining his undisputed ownership of the title.

It was Welshman Brian Curvis's last appearance on 12 September 1966 in a bout that took place at the Market Hall in Carmarthen, Wales. The opponent facing the reigning British welterweight and Commonwealth king in the ten-round non-title bout was Northern Ireland's future British super-lightweight champion Des Rea. The contest was halted in round eight in Curvis's favour; it saw him bow out of the sport after comprising a record of forty-one fights of which he won thirty-seven and lost four. During his career, Curvis failed to win the world crown in his division, being outpointed over

Muhammad Ali (left), seen with entertainer Sammy Davis Jr and Drew Bundini Brown, was the first world heavyweight champion to defend his title against challengers who fought in a southpaw stance. (*Derek Rowe*)

fifteen rounds on 22 September 1964 by defending champion Emile Griffith of the Virgin Islands. The fight took place at the Empire Pool in Wembley, London. Curvis also failed in his bid to add the European title to his name when he retired in round fourteen of fifteen for the vacant championship against Frenchman Jean Josselin. This contest took place on 25 April 1966 at the Palais des Sports in Paris, France. However, Curvis created a record during his career of being the first man in his weight division to win two Lonsdale Belts outright for making defences of the British crown; this meant that the Welshman won six title bouts to own the two belts. Curvis even put a notch on a third belt when he achieved a seventh British title victory.

Scotland's Walter McGowan made the first defence of his lineal, EBU, New York, and British world flyweight title on 30 December 1966 at the Kittikachorn Stadium in Bangkok, Thailand, against Chartchai Chionoi. McGowan started the contest well, looking the more superior boxer of the two, much to the anguish of Chioni's many supporters who were giving him a great deal of vocal support. The tough challenger refused to wilt and in round nine of fifteen, the championship changed hands when McGowan was stopped with a bad nose injury. This was the first time that a British fighter had contested a world title fight in Thailand.

When the fight was first announced, it looked to be one which would produce its share of excitement between two men who had excellent ring skills. The contest was going to take place at Madison Square Garden in New York. The event was the world middleweight title bout with defending champion Emile Griffith of the Virgin Islands making the third defence of his crown against Nino Benvenuti. It was generally felt that Griffith would still be champion when the bout was over. On 17 April 1967, a surprise occurred. After fifteen rounds in which both combatants gave their very all, the title changed hands. Benvenuti was awarded the decision on points. This was a great victory for Benvenuti who became the first Italian born boxer to win this title.

Ken Buchanan entered the Ice Rink in Paisley, Scotland, on 11 May 1967 and up to that time had done everything right in his professional career, earning an undefeated record of eighteen bouts. Now it was time to take that vital step up in class and the man to examine his credentials was Italy's Franco Brondi, a fighter who was most experienced with a résumé of thirty-eight bouts (winning thirty-three and losing five). Brondi was also a former European lightweight champion, so a win over this opponent would be a good victory for the Scot. A solid ten-round points win would be good, but Buchanan excelled by stopping Brondi in the third session, further confirming his potential as a champion of the future.

When Ken Buchanan (the future world British and European lightweight champion) ducked between the ropes to enter the ring at

Ken Buchanan confirmed that he was a force to be reckoned with by defeating Italy's Franco Brondi in 1967. (*Derek Rowe*)

the Afan Lido Sports Centre in Aberavon, Wales, on 26 July 1967 to do battle with Frenchman Rene Roque, a win for the talented Scot was the expected result. Buchanan came into the contest with an undefeated résumé of twenty fights while Roque came in to the foray with a slate of thirty fights, three defeats, and four draws. As expected, Buchanan boxed his way to a ten-round points victory over his opponent to further confirm his potential. Yet few realised at the time that Buchanan's victory over his opponent was a better win than first thought since Roque proved to be a solid performer and was by no means a pushover. On 22 April 1970, he travelled to Italy to take on former world super-lightweight-king Sandro Lopopolo for the vacant European super-lightweight belt. Lopopolo, the local favourite, looked set to add this title to his name at the Montecatini Terme in Toscana, Italy, in front of his home fans. A win here for the championship would have put Lopopolo back in the main stream of the division. Roque, however, had over ideas; he too had ambitions and produced the boxing skills to outpoint his rival over fifteen rounds to lift the title—a shock result. Roque showed that this victory was by no means a fluke as he successfully defended this championship on four occasions until he came up against former European and future WBC lightweight king Pedro Carrasco of Spain on 21 May 1971. Roque entered his opponent's territory at the Palacio de los Deportes in Madrid, Spain, and lost a fifteen-round points decision. Roque may have lost the title, but he can take consolation from the fact that he was beaten by one of the best fighters in action at that time.

Only one man in the history of UK boxing has won three Lonsdale Belts outright for defending the British title; that honour belongs to Henry Cooper, who accomplished this feat on 7 November 1967 at the Empire Pool in Wembley, London, stopping challenger Billy Walker in round six of fifteen. To win one Lonsdale Belt outright, a boxer had to win three title fights. Henry thus amazingly won nine championship fights to win the three belts. The rule later changed, hence a boxer must now win four title bouts to win the belt outright and only one belt may be won in any respective weight division.

Yves Desmarets, who was the featherweight champion of France, had his last professional bout on 22 December 1967, losing to Spanish fighter Jose Legra for the vacant European title, being stopped in the third round of a scheduled fifteen at the Madrid Comunidad de Madrid in Spain. Desmarets left the boxing scene with a record of thirty-three fights (winning thirty, losing two, and drawing one). The respective draw took place on 31 January 1964 when Desmarets fought a fifteen-round draw when defending the featherweight championship of France against challenger Antoine Martin at the Toulouse Haute-Garonne. The first professional

Henry Cooper made history by being the first man to win three Lonsdale Belts outright.
(*Derek Rowe*)

defeat for Desmarets came at the hands of Welshman Howard Winstone on 22 January 1965 when challenging for the European featherweight title at the Palazzetto dello Sport in Rome, Italy, resulting in a fifteen-point victory for Winstone. The only two defeats came in challenges for the European title against two boxers who went on to win a version of the world crown at the weight: Winstone (WBC) and Legra (twice WBC).

Even after losing the tips off of three of his fingers on his right hand in an accident at work, Welshman Howard Winstone showed a fighting spirit to overcome this disadvantage and carve out an outstanding career in the professional ranks, winning not just the British and European titles, but also the world featherweight crown. To become king of the division, Winstone stopped Japan's Mitsunori Seki at the Royal Albert Hall in Kensington, London, for the vacant WBC championship on 23 January 1968 in round nine of fifteen; this was the Welshman's fourth attempt at a world championship. Previous challenges took place on 7 September 1965 against Mexico's Vicente Saldivar—a man destined to be ranked with the greats in the division. Winstone gave the Mexican a difficult night and fought every inch of the way in his attempt to gain global championship status but lost a fifteen-round points decision at the Earls Court Arena in Kensington, London. On 15 June 1967, Winstone shared the ring for the second time with Saldivar at Ninian Park in Cardiff, Wales, and raised his game to an even higher level than in his attempt to grab the crown. It was a case of the matador and the bull with Winstone the matador spearing the attacks of the bull (Saldivar) with his immaculate left jab, which constantly found its target. Despite his magnificent effort, Winstone could not deter Saldivar who would not be denied he kept coming forward throwing punches of his own from a southpaw stance. After a thrilling encounter that kept those in attendance on the edge of their seats, Winstone lost a close fifteen-round points decision. The third attempt took place on 14 October 1967 in a contest that saw the saw Welsh fighter travel to the Estadio Azteca in Mexico City. Winstone seemed to have very little chance of victory in this meeting; if he could not defeat the Mexican on home turf, how was he going to defeat the champion in his own backyard? He also had to deal with the high altitude of the country. Winstone put in a brave performance but suffered defeat when stopped by Saldivar in round twelve of fifteen. The subsequent and indeed surprising retirement of Saldivar opened the door for the Welshman's winning attempt at the crown against Mitsunori Seki. Winstone did not have a long reign since he lost the title in his first defence, which took place on 24 July 1968. The venue was the Coney Beach Arena in Porthcawl, Wales, which saw Winstone stopped in round five of a scheduled fifteen by Jose Legra, a Cuban-born fighter but a citizen of Spain. Winstone had previously defeated Legra on 22 June 1965 by way of a ten-round points decision at the Winter Gardens in Blackpool, Lancashire. Howard duly retired in 1969 after comprising a record of sixty-seven bouts with sixty-one victories and six defeats.

It was the changing of the guard on 19 February 1968 when Ken Buchanan took to the ring to challenge Maurice Cullen for the British lightweight crown at the Hilton Hotel in Mayfair, London. Cullen from Shotton, Tyne and Wear, was an experienced fighter with a record tally of forty wins, five defeats, and two draws; he would thus be making the fourth defence of his title against his domestic opponent. Buchanan confirmed his promise as a fighter with a future when he extended his undefeated record to twenty-four by knocking out Cullen in round eleven of a scheduled fifteen and hence became the first Scottish boxer since Seaman Nobby Hall (who reigned from 1922–23) to acquire this championship.

Jimmy Anderson became the first holder of the British super-featherweight title on 20 February 1968. After a hard-fought battle, he produced the finishing blow and stopped southpaw opponent Jimmy Revie in round nine of fifteen at the Royal Albert Hall in London. Coming into the battle, Revie was undefeated in thirteen bouts with every win having taken place inside

From left to right: Maurice Cullen, Howard Winstone, and Ken Buchanan, who had just defeated Cullen for the British lightweight crown in 1968. (*Derek Rowe*)

the distance so it was evident that he could bang a bit. Anderson too was known as a big puncher with a record of twenty-seven fights, twenty ending inside the scheduled distance, with five defeats. Even before the first bell had sounded to start the fifteen-round contest, it was clear that the odds of this fight going the full distance of fifteen rounds was to say the least very remote.

Manager Terry Lawless from London scored an excellent double on 20 February 1968 since two of his charges battled their way to a British championship. Not only did Jimmy Anderson bring a domestic title to the Lawless stable, but Ralph Charles fought his way to the British and Commonwealth welterweight championship, outscoring defending champion Johnny Cooke over fifteen rounds. In the years to follow, Lawless would take a number of fighters to various titles (the world, British, European, and Commonwealth), making him one of the most successful boxing managers from the UK.

Australian Lionel Rose stamped his name in the boxing record books on 27 February 1968 when he travelled to Japan to challenge defending world bantamweight title-holder Fighting Hara at the Nippon Budokan in Tokyo. At first sight, it appeared that the defence by Harada (also a former holder of the world flyweight crown) would be another successful outing for the champion. The Japanese boxer had turned back four previous challengers: Alan Rudkin (England), Eder Jofre (Brazil; the fighter who Harada defeated to take the title), Jose Medel (Mexico), and Bernardo Caraballo (Columbia). However, despite all the odds being stacked against him by fighting on the champion's home ground, Rose boxed his way to a fifteen-round points decision and became the first Aboriginal Australian to win a world boxing crown.

In the inaugural contest for the British super-lightweight championship, which took place at York Hall in Bethnal Green, London, on 27 February 1968, Des Rea boxed his way to championship status when attaining a fifteen-round points decision over opponent Vic Andreetti to claim the crown and to be always remembered as the first champion at the weight. Prior to the contest, the experienced Andreetti looked as if he might know a little too much for his opponent, entering the ring with a record of fifty-eight bouts (winning forty-six, losing nine, and drawing three). Against that, Rea had a slate of twenty-one fights (winning fourteen, losing five, and drawing two of his professional fights).

During his tenure as European middleweight champion, Italian resident Juan Carlos Duran (who was born in Argentina) made a defence against two challengers from the UK, both of which he won on a disqualification. The first occasion took place on 26 March 1968 against former British welterweight and middleweight champion Wally Swift, whose bid for the crown came to an abrupt end in round ten of a fifteen-round contest when he was disqualified for headbutting; at the time, he looked to be heading for victory. The venue for the bout was the Embassy Sportsdome in Birmingham, West Midlands. The next Brit trying his luck was Johnny Pritchett the reigning British and Commonwealth champion, who had to travel to the Palazzo dello Sport in Milan, Italy, on 20 February 1969 for his shot. Pritchett lasted longer than his countryman, getting into the thirteenth round of a scheduled fifteen when disaster struck with the referee disqualifying him for a headbutt. At the time, Pritchett was well in command of the fight and looked to be coasting to a point's victory.

Against all odds, at the 1968 Mexican Olympic Games, the UK's Chris Finnegan found his rainbow when he fought his way through tough competition to reach the final. In so doing, Finnegan outpointed Soviet Union's Aleksei Kiselyov to take the gold medal in the middleweight division. Finnegan became the first Briton to win this colour medal in the division since Harry Mallin, who won gold at the 1924 Games in Paris by defeating fellow Brit John Elliott on points.

Chris Finnegan proudly
wearing his gold medal,
which he won at the
1968 Mexico Olympic
Games. (*Derek Rowe*)

Italy's Sandro Mazzinghi became the first fighter to regain the WBA world super-welterweight title on 26 May 1968 when he outpointed defending champion Ki-Soon Kim of South Korea over fifteen rounds at the San Siro in Milan, Italy. Mazzinghi previously held the title from 1963–1965; Kim had won the championship from one Italian in the shape of Nino Benvenuti on 25 June 1966, only to lose it in his third defence to another.

Tom Bogs became the first Danish boxer to win a European title in two different weight divisions. On 12 September 1968, he made short work of defending European light-heavyweight champion Lothar Stengel at the Idraetsparken in Copenhagen, Denmark, stopping his German opponent in the first of a scheduled fifteen-round contest. After making a successful defence of the crown, Bogs dropped down to the middleweight division and challenged the European king at the poundage Juan Carlos Duran of Italy on 11 September 1969. The venue being the Idraetsparken in Copenhagen, Bogs captured his second European crown, winning a fifteen-round points decision to become the new champion. After making three successful defences of the title, Bogs paid a visit to Italy on 4 December 1970 and lost the crown in a return to Juan Carlos Duran losing a fifteen-round points decision. Bogs became the champion once again at the weight when he fought Italian Fabio Bettini for the vacant title, winning a fifteen-round points verdict at the K. B. Hallen in Copenhagen on 18 January 1973.

Shozo Saijo brought a version of the world featherweight title to Japan for the first time on 27 September 1968. Saijo travelled to the Memorial Coliseum in Los Angeles, California, to make his bid against American Raul Rojas. Rojas had previously lost to Saijo over ten rounds in a non-title bout on 6 June 1968 in a contest which took place at the Olympic Auditorium in Los Angeles, California. Rojas was making the first defence of the WBA crown and many felt that this time, he would get the better of his Japanese challenger but they were wrong. After fifteen rounds, the decision went to Saijo who boxed extremely well to take the championship.

During his career, Nigerian-born Santos Martins met two future British world champions in their respective debut in the professional ranks. On 30 October 1968, he squared up to future WBC world lightweight champion Jim Watt at the Town Hall in Hamilton and said goodnight when he was knocked out by the Scot in round four of a six round contest. John H. Stracey from London was the next future world title-holder (WBC welterweight) to be met by Martins when climbing into the ring to fight for pay for the first time on 17 September 1969. The venue was the York Hall at Bethnal Green in London. Stracey vanquished Martins quicker than Watt and had his arm held up in victory when knocking out his opponent in round two of a bout slated for six.

Former world heavyweight contender Thad Spencer fought four times in the UK during his professional career. Spencer's last contest in Britain took place on 12 November 1968 at the Empire Pool. On this occasion, the visitor from the USA was stopped in six of a ten-round contest by Billy Walker. Spencer first boxed in Britain on 18 April 1966 at the King's Hall, Belle Vue, in Manchester in a bout made over ten rounds against future European, British, and Commonwealth heavyweight champion Jack Bodell. The bout proved successful when Bodell retired in round two. Spencer returned to the Kings Hall on 2 May 1966 against former British and Commonwealth heavyweight king Brian London and once again put another win on his record when he boxed his way to a ten-round points decision. At the Royal Albert Hall in London on 28 May 1968, Spencer went to war with fellow countryman Leotis Martin in a contest that proved to be a thrilling encounter between two hard-hitting fighters. Spencer was stopped in the ninth round of ten when the referee stepped in to halt the proceedings.

The 1968 Olympic middleweight gold medal winner Chris Finnegan made a winning start to his highly anticipated professional career on 9 December 1968 at the Hilton Hotel, Mayfair, London, stopping his opponent Mike Fleetham in the third round of a scheduled six.

Manager Sam Burns (left) with Chris Finnegan, who is seen signing a contract to join the professional ranks. (*Derek Rowe*)

Scottish-born Jimmy Bell had eked out a successful professional boxing career in Australia, being undefeated in eighteen fights (winning seventeen and drawing one). The draw took place in Japan. So it was somewhat ironic that in his first paid bout in his homeland on 11 December 1968, he should unexpectedly lose his undefeated record to fellow countryman Bobby Fisher. Fisher defeated Bell by way of an eight-round points decision. The contest took place at the Town Hall in Hamilton, Scotland.

American Don Fullmer attempted to emulate his older brother Gene by challenging Italian Nino Benvenuti for the world middleweight title on 14 December 1968. Gene Fullmer had twice held the world crown in this division during his career. However, the Fullmer family was not going to get their hands on his championship again for at the Teatro Ariston in Sanremo, Italy, Benvenuti boxed his way to a fifteen-round points decision to retain the crown despite being put down for a count in round seven.

On 21 January 1969, Australian Johnny Famechon succeeded where his uncle Ray failed when at the Royal Albert Hall in London, he outpointed reigning WBC world featherweight king Jose Legra (a Cuban-born citizen of Spain) over fifteen rounds to capture the world crown. Frenchman Ray had challenged for the undisputed featherweight title on 17 March 1950 at

Madison Square Garden in New York, but failed in his bid when outpointed over fifteen rounds by the defending champion, Willie Pep of America—a man considered to be one of the greats in the division. Following his victory over Legra, Famechon became a frequent visitor to the UK, having a further four non-title bouts in the country. On 21 April 1969, he showed his boxing skills by outpointing Italian Giovanni Girgenti over ten rounds at the Hilton Hotel (The Angelo American Sporting Club) in Mayfair, London. This was an interesting match since Famechon and Girgenti were no strangers to each other, having met twice before. In their first pairing on 9 December 1966 in Australia at the Festival Hall, they fought to a ten-round draw. In a return on 20 January 1967 at the same location, Famechon took a ten-round decision on points. On 20 May 1969, Famechon stepped between the ropes to face the hard-punching British super-featherweight champion Jimmy Anderson—always a dangerous opponent for anyone inside the ring. The Briton pressed the world champion hard, but the Australian champion breezed through the contest, taking a deserved ten-round decision over his foe at the Royal Albert Hall. It was back to the same venue on 11 November 1969 where Famechon clocked up another ten-round points decision over Miguel Herrera of Ecuador. Fighting at the Royal Albert Hall must have been like a second home to Famechon for once again on 9 December 1969, he went to work at this venue for the fourth time and while not known as a concussive puncher, he put the lights out for opponent Pete Gonzalez of America, who was knocked out in the third session of a ten-round contest. This bout was Famechon's last appearance inside a British ring.

Beryl Cameron-Gibbons, who hailed from London, made her mark in boxing when in 1969, she became one of the few woman in the United Kingdom to be granted a licence by the British Boxing Board of Control to be a promoter.

At the Midlands Sporting Club in Solihull, West Midlands, on 7 May 1969, Tony Barlow from Manchester failed in his attempt to capture the British flyweight crown from Scotland's defending champion John McCluskey when stopped in round thirteen of fifteen. This was the fourth meeting between the two in the professional ranks and on each occasion, Barlow met with defeat. They first crossed gloves on 1 November 1965 at the Hilton Hotel, Mayfair, when McCluskey stopped Barlow in eighth and last round. The pair resumed hostilities at the Kings Hall in Belle Vue in Manchester, Lancashire on 2 May 1966. Once again, the Scot came out on top when stopped Barlow in round five of a scheduled eight. At the Free Trade Hall in Manchester in a contest for the then-vacant British flyweight crown on 16 January 1967, Barlow was unable to score that elusive victory over the Scot when he suffered defeat when knocked out in round eight of fifteen by McCluskey.

Right: Danny Holland (left) with Beryl Cameron-Gibbons. (*Derek Rowe*)

Below: *From left to right*: manager Doug Bidwell, Beryl Cameron-Gibbons (who became one of the few woman to become a licensed promoter with the British Boxing Board of Control), future world middleweight champion Alan Minter, and renowned trainer Danny Holland. (*Derek Rowe*)

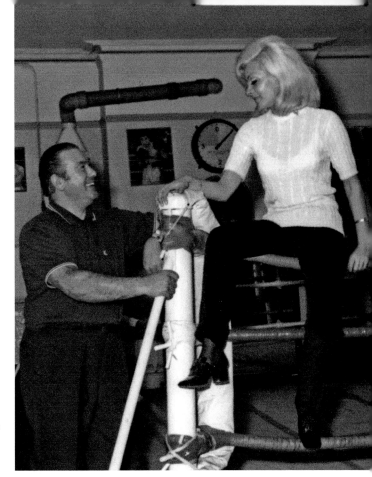

Johnny Famechon of Australia made a successful defence of his WBC world featherweight title on 28 July 1969 against challenger Fighting Harada of Japan, who was bidding to win a world crown in a third weight division. Harada a former world flyweight and bantamweight king battled hard to acquire the championship and travelled the full fifteen rounds in his attempt but came up short losing the decision on points. The contest took place at the Sydney Stadium in Australia. The referee in charge of the bout was more than familiar to the weight division as he was the legendary former two-time world featherweight great Willie Pep of America.

From left to right: Howard Winstone, Reg Gutteridge (boxing journalist and TV commentator), and former world featherweight champion Willie Pep (who refereed the Famechon *v*. Harada world featherweight title bout). (*Derek Rowe*)

6

Round Six: 1970–1979

Ken Buchanan's first professional contest abroad did not end too well for him on 29 January 1970. Buchanan contested the vacant European lightweight title against Miguel Velazquez at the Palacio de los Deportes, Comunidad de Madrid in Spain. Buchanan got into the ring with an undefeated record of thirty-three bouts and his rival Valazquez came in with an impressive résumé of thirty-eight wins, one draw, and one defeat. While it was not going to be a walkover for Buchanan against his Spanish opponent, it was felt that the Scot had the class to take the title. However, it was not Buchanan's night as he was floored for a count in round nine and lost a fifteen-round points decision along with his undefeated record. Buchanan had boxed better in past fights it must be said; however, many felt that he was a little unlucky not to have taken the victory. Interestingly, both would go on to win a world title: Buchanan the undisputed lightweight championship and Velazquez the WBC super-lightweight crown.

On 6 April 1970, Welshman Eddie Avoth made a successful defence of his British light-heavyweight crown against former holder of the title, Young McCormack from Northern Ireland, at the Ice Rink, Nottingham. McCormack failed in his attempt to regain the championship when disqualified in round eight of a scheduled fifteen for illegal use of his head. The contest saw for the first time the same two boxers fighting three times for the domestic title in this division. Avoth and McCormack exchanged punches for the championship on 19 June 1967 at the National Sporting Club, Piccadilly. On that occasion, the two met for the vacant belt whereupon McCormack emerged victorious stopping Avoth in the seventh session of a fifteen-round bout. At the Anglo-American Sporting Club in Mayfair, London, on 13 January 1969, McCormack and Avoth renewed their fighting acquaintance for the second time; once again, the contest failed to go the full fifteen rounds when McCormack retired in round eleven, hence losing the title to Avoth.

It was something of a shock when Bunny Sterling defeated the reigning champion Mark Rowe for the British and Commonwealth middleweight titles. The respective bout took place at the Empire Pool in London on 8 September 1970. While Sterling was a respected opponent, it was felt that Rowe (with a record of thirty fights: winning twenty-seven and losing three) would remain king of the division in the UK when the battle concluded. Then Rowe would go on to fight for higher honours. In short, Rowe's challenger was just an obstacle who needed to be overcome. Sterling had participated in twenty-seven bouts (winning sixteen, losing nine, with two drawn). The fight was halted in the fourth session in favour of Sterling in a match set for fifteen rounds with Rowe suffering facial cuts. History was made on the night since Jamaican-born Sterling became the first black immigrant to win a British championship.

It was an incredible victory when Ken Buchanan of Scotland outpointed defending champion Ismael Laguna over fifteen rounds at the Hiram Bithorn Stadium in San Juan, Puerto Rico, on 26 September 1970 to capture the WBA world lightweight crown. It was one of those situations that often occur in boxing whereby many pundits wrote the Scot's chances off since he had all the odds stacked against him. Yet Ken showed that he was a class act by not just overcoming an excellent champion in the shape of Laguna, but also the overwhelming oppressive heat that he had to endure during the battle. The ring was in the open air, which did not help the Scot's cause; however, Buchanan showed the heart of a champion to take the title in a hard-fought encounter. Chic Calderwood, another Scottish boxer, contested a world title in San Juan on 15 October 1966 and at this very same venue suffered a two-round knockout of a scheduled fifteen when up against the very formidable defending world light-heavyweight champion Jose Torres. Buchanan became the first boxer from the UK to hold a version of the lightweight crown since Welsh Freddie Welsh, who reigned from 1914–1917. However, since the British Boxing Board of Control was affiliated to the WBC and not the WBA, he was not officially recognised in his own country.

During his career, heavyweight Danny McAlinden may not have fought any boxer who either held or went on to win the world championship in his division. However, he did cross gloves with two fighters whose brothers did win the ultimate prize at the weight. On 3 December 1970, McAlinden drew over ten rounds with American Ray Patterson at the Civic Hall, Wolverhampton. Ray was the younger brother of Floyd Patterson, who was not only a world champion but the first man in the history of the sport to

Howard Winstone (left) with Eddie Avoth, who met Young McCormack three times for the British light-heavyweight crown. (*Derek Rowe*)

From left to right: Eddie Thomas with Ken Buchanan (who overcame the odds to win the WBA world lightweight crown), speaking to then Prime Minister Edward Heath and Reg Gutteridge. (*Derek Rowe*)

Above left: Princess Anne (left) with Ken Buchanan, who shows that his footwork outside of the ring is also excellent on the dance floor. (*Derek Rowe*)

Above right: Danny McAlinden enjoyed a degree of success when boxing the brothers of world heavyweight champions. (*Derek Rowe*)

regain the world heavyweight crown. Then on 8 March 1971, the Irish-born fighter ventured to the USA and at Madison Square Garden in New York outpointed Rahman Ali over six rounds. Rahman was the younger brother of boxing great Muhammad Ali, who among his many achievements in the ring became the first man to regain the heavyweight title twice.

Billy Backus of America pulled off a massive upset when he stopped Mexico's Jose Napoles in four rounds of fifteen to unexpectedly capture the world welterweight championship. A cut eye was the cause of the stoppage at the War Memorial Auditorium in Syracuse on 3 December 1970. In so doing, Backus emulated his uncle Carmen Basilio, who won the same title on 10 June 1955. A return bout with Napoles took place at the Inglewood Forum in Los Angeles on 4 June 1971. Many felt that Backus would concede the title back to the former champion; he did this when Naploles regained the crown, stopping the American in round eight of fifteen.

At the YMCA Hall in Canberra on 12 December 1970, Australian Capital Terrioty Toro George battled Ken Braddley for the vacant Commonwealth featherweight title and was victorious when the bout was stopped in the sixth round of fifteen to see him become the first fighter from New Zealand to hold this crown.

Italy's Tommaso Galli of Italy became the first holder of the European super-featherweight crown on 13 January 1971. The contest for the inaugural title against Spain's Luisa Aisa took place at the Ladispoli Lazio in Italy. The bout went the scheduled fifteen rounds with the points decision going in the favour of the home fighter. Galli was clearly a force to be reckoned with on the continent, also being a former European, bantamweight, and featherweight title-holder.

Canada's Bill Drover (born in Scotland) was a frequent visitor to the UK, testing the top heavyweights in Britain at the time. Drover made what could be considered a bright start in his first British outing, earning a ten-round draw against future British, European, and Commonwealth heavyweight champion Joe Bugner at the York Hall in Bethnal Green, London, on 10 February 1971. Drover showed in the Bugner bout that he was good value and was not a walkover opponent. However, his next five bouts were not so successful. Jack Bodell (the future British, European, and Commonwealth title-holder) outpointed him over ten rounds at the Royal Albert Hall in London on 27 April 1971. Another future champion, Danny McAlinden, who would go on to win the British and Commonwealth titles, met Drover at the Grosvenor House in Mayfair, London, the outcome being a four-round knockout victory for the home fighter. The bout was scheduled for ten.

Future WBC world, British, European, and Commonwealth light-heavyweight champion John Conteh was the next to share the ring with Drover. Conteh was boxing at heavyweight at that time. The bout, which was set for ten rounds, took place at the Royal Albert Hall, Kensington; it finished in the seventh session with Conteh scoring a knockout. Drover returned to the Royal Albert Hall on 16 January 1973 to meet Les Stevens, finishing on the wrong side of an eight-round points decision. On 22 October 1973, at the Grosvenor House in Mayfair, London, Drover was in action again; this time in the opposite corner was future British light-heavyweight king Tim Wood, who took the decision on points after eight rounds. The bout against Woods proved to be Drover's last professional contest; he eventually departed from the sport with a record of fifty-two bouts (winning thirty-three, losing sixteen, and drawing three).

On 12 February 1971, Scotland's Ken Buchanan made the first defence of his WBA world lightweight title against American Ruben Navarro at the Sports Arena in Los Angeles, California; he won a fifteen-round points decision. The original opponent for Buchanan on this date was another fighter from the USA, former world lightweight king Mando Ramos, who pulled out of the contest. While Navarro may not have been considered as good as Ramos, he proved a worthy opponent, pushing the Scot hard in the early stages of the contest before being defeated. Since the WBC also recognised the contest as being for their vacant championship, Buchanan hence became the undisputed champion. Buchanan was later stripped of the WBC version of the title within a few months for agreeing to fight former champion Ismael Laguna of Panama rather than that organisation's mandatory challenger, Pedro Carrasco of Spain.

At Madison Square Garden in New York on 8 March 1971, two undefeated records were destroyed. These belonged to Muhammad Ali and his younger brother, Rahman Ali. Muhammad lost a fifteen-round points decision in his bid to regain the world heavyweight crown against reigning title-holder Joe Frazier. Going into the battle, Ali had a slate of thirty-one wins to his credit with no defeats. Frazier entered the bout also undefeated in twenty-six bouts. On the undercard, Rahman was outpointed over six rounds by Ireland's Danny McAlinden (the future British and Commonwealth heavyweight champion). McAlinden's record was comprised of fourteen victories one defeat and two draws, with Rahman's standing at a perfect seven. It was not a good night for the Ali family.

On 29 April 1971, Italy's Carmelo Bossi defended his WBA world super-welterweight title against Spain's Jose Hernandez at the Palacio de los Deportes in Madrid, Spain. The contest went the full fifteen rounds and for the first time in this weight division, a world championship contest ended in a draw.

Juan Carlos Duran of Italy came off second best in his defence of the European middleweight crown in Paris on 9 June 1971 when outpointed over fifteen rounds by French title-holder Jean Claude Bouttier. This proved to be the last time that Duran would contest the championship in this division. However, Duran had the distinctive at that time of participating in more European title bouts at middleweight than any other fighter (eight times).

Chris Finnegan added the European crown to his British and Commonwealth light-heavyweight titles when he outpointed holder Conny Velensek over fifteen rounds at the Ice Rink in Nottingham on 1 February 1972. This was the second meeting between the two fighters for the championship. The British boxer had previously challenged the Slovenia-born German title-holder for the crown on 5 May 1971 at the Deutschlandhalle in Charlottenburg, Berlin, West Germany. On that occasion, the contest was declared a draw after fifteen rounds, allowing Velensek to keep the title in his grasp. Many were of the view that Finnegan

Ken Buchanan proved he was the top man in the lightweight division when he became undisputed world champion in 1971, adding the WBC crown to his already-held WBA version of the title. (*Derek Rowe*)

was somewhat unlucky not to have come home as the new champion. On winning the championship, Finnegan became the first fighter from the UK to hold the title since Don Cockell, who reigned from 1951 to 1952. The bout between Velensek and Finnegan was the first European light-heavyweight title contest to end in a draw since 1 December 1937, when Belgium's Gustave Roth fought fellow countryman Karel Sys in a scheduled fifteen-round contest at the Bruxelles-Capitale in Brussels. Their meeting was also recognised by the IBU as a world championship bout for the crown held by Roth.

During his career, American Eddie Duncan proved to be a handful for British fighters. On 12 June 1972, he came to the UK to meet future British light-heavyweight champion Johnny Frankham at the Hilton Hotel in Mayfair, London. Duncan surprised many by holding Frankham to a draw over eight rounds. Duncan came back to meet John Conteh, a man considered a hot prospect; a win for the Briton looked assured at the Empire Pool on 26 September 1972, but Duncan once again surprised by earning a ten-round points decision. Conteh lived up to expectations and went on to win the WBC world, European, British, and Commonwealth light-heavyweight titles. Phil Matthews was the next to exchange punches with Duncan at the Grosvenor House, Mayfair on 19 February 1973 and finished second when losing a ten-round points decision. Duncan appeared to be a danger man for British boxers so when he returned again to the UK on 11 October 1973 to meet Maxie Smith at the Kings Hall, Belle Vue, you had to wonder if he was going to be victorious once again. However, Smith restored British pride when he came out on top and won a decision on points over ten rounds.

Ken Buchanan lost the WBA world lightweight title in his third defence at Madison Square Garden in New York on 26 June 1972, being stopped in round thirteen of fifteen by Panama's Roberto Duran. Buchanan had taken the crown from Ismael Laguna with a fifteen round points decision on 26 September 1970 at the Hiram Bithorn Stadium in San Juan, Puerto Rico. It was ironic that Buchanan should win the championship from one Panamanian boxer only to lose it to another fighter from the same country.

It makes you wonder if it is wise to have two boxing siblings compete on the same card in a big fight, sometimes it works out, sometimes it does not.

John Conteh found defeat for the first time in the professional ranks when outpointed by American Eddie Duncan in 1972. (*Derek Rowe*)

It certainly did not go to well for the Quarry brothers on 27 June 1972 at the Convention Center, Las Vegas. Younger brother Mike stepped into the ring to challenge fellow American Bob Foster for the undisputed world light-heavyweight crown in a contest set for fifteen rounds. Quarry lost his bid for the championship and his undefeated record, which then stood at thirty-five bouts when he was felled for the full count in round four. Later, big brother Jerry entered the fray to challenge former undisputed world heavyweight title-holder Muhammad Ali for the NABF heavyweight trinket. Quarry had previously lost to Ali on 26 October 1970 at the City Auditorium in Atlanta, Georgia, when he duly retired in round three of a fifteen-round contest. Jerry once again met with defeat at the hands of Ali when he was stopped in the seventh session of a contest set for twelve.

Jose Hernandez of Spain lost his European super-welterweight crown in his fourth defence on 5 July 1972. The battle for European supremacy took place at San Remo, Italy. Challenger Juan Carlos Duran, fighting in front of his home fans, boxed his way to a fifteen-round points decision to take the title. The notable aspect of the occasion was that Duran became the first former holder of the European middleweight championship to drop down a division to win this title.

On 13 September 1972, Rahman Ali went up against fellow American Jack O'Halloran in a contest set for the duration of ten rounds in San Diego, California. The brother of former world heavyweight king Muhammad Ali, Rahman failed to last the distance when he was knocked out in the eighth round. This was the last professional appearance by Ali, who quit the ring with a record of eighteen fights (winning fourteen, losing three, and drawing one.)

Despite home ground advantage, Joey Santos failed to become the first holder of the Commonwealth super-lightweight crown when Joe Tetteh of Ghana stopped him in round ten of fifteen to claim the vacant title at the Town Hall in Wellington, New Zealand, on 21 September 1972. Santos looked the likely winner of this contest when the fight was signed, but Tetteh, who was often underrated during his career, took the victory. Tetteh went into the fifteen-round contest with a wealth of experience behind him after taking part in seventy-one fights (winning forty-four, losing twenty-two, and drawing five). The record of Santos looked a little pale when compared with his opponents having participated in twenty-two fights with just the sole defeat. The contest with Santos was Tetteh's second crack at a Commonwealth title. On 5 October 1963, he challenged fellow countryman Floyd Robertson for the featherweight crown at the Accra Sports Stadium in Ghana, being stopped in round eleven of a scheduled fifteen.

Australia's Charkey Ramon put on a show for his fans on 30 October 1972, etching his name into the record books by becoming the first holder

of the Commonwealth super-welterweight title. Ramon accomplished
this feat when he stopped England's Pat Dwyer at the Festival Hall in
Melbourne, Australia, by way of a stoppage in round eight of a bout set
for fifteen. Going into the battle, Ramon's record stood at twenty-eight
fights, one defeat, one draw. Dwyer's slate was forty-three fights with
thirty-three wins, eight defeats, and two draws.

Germany's Rudiger Schmidtke did the unexpected on 14 November
1972 when he travelled to the UK to challenge holder Chris Finnegan
at the Empire Pool in London for the European light-heavyweight title.
This was Schmidtke's second crack at the title, having lost a fifteen-round
points decision to the then holder of the championship, Italy's Piero Del
Papa, on 11 September 1970. The contest took place in Frankfurt in
Germany. On his second attempt, few expected Schmidtke to be any more
successful; however, the challenger acquired the title when he stopped
Finnegan in round twelve of a fifteen round contest. Schmidtke returned
to the UK to make the first defence of his title on 13 March 1973 against
John Conteh at the same venue where he first captured the crown. In his
second visit to British shores, Schmidtke did not do so well as he lost the
title ironically in the same session in which he won it round twelve. The
bout was scheduled for fifteen rounds, but it was obvious the way Conteh
was venomously attacking his man that the contest would not go the full
distance.

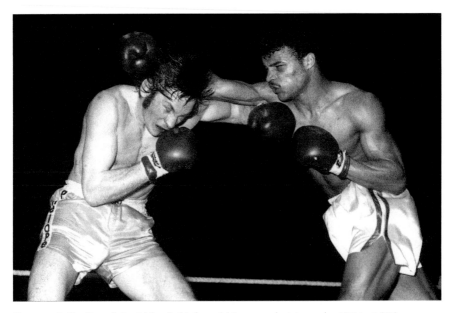

Germany's Rudiger Schmidtke (left) found his second visit to the UK in 1973 was not
as pleasant as his first when he found John Conteh far too hot to handle. (*Derek Rowe*)

The man seemed to be unbeatable in the ring but Puerto Rican Esteban de Jesús disproved that fact on 17 November 1972 at Madison Square Garden, New York, when he outpointed the reigning WBA world lightweight king Roberto Duran over ten rounds. Their meeting was a non-title affair with Duran coming into the contest with an undefeated record of thirty-one fights. De Jesús was no easy touch, entering the bout with a résumé of thirty-four fights with one defeat. Despite the impressive record, the result was a surprise as no one expected de Jesús to score a victory. The win was a golden bonus for de Jesús; it elevated him in the rankings, making him a major name and a man to contend with. The pair met again on 16 March 1974 at the Gimnasio Nuevo, Panama City. This time, Duran was putting his WBA world lightweight championship on the line and extracted sweet revenge when, in a fifteen-round contest, he knocked out de Jesús in the eleventh round. There had to be a third contest between the two men; this took place on 21 January 1978 at Caesars Palace, Las Vegas. The bout was a unification contest; after losing to Duran, de Jesús fought his way back to being a contender and was rewarded on 8 May 1976 by getting a shot at Guts Ishimatsu, the Japanese WBC world lightweight champion. The two fighters fought at the Juan Ramón Loubriel Stadium in Bayamón, Puerto Rico, and de Jesús won a fifteen-round decision to take the title. De Jesús was confident that he would emerge the undisputed champion at the end of the scheduled meeting with Duran. However, Duran proved supreme and ended the championship bout by a knockout in round twelve of fifteen.

On 29 January 1973, the spectators at the Albany Hotel in Glasgow may not have realised it at the time, but they were not only watching a former world lightweight champion in action but also another boxer who would one day rule the world. The contest in question was the challenge for the British lightweight crown by former world and British lightweight champion Ken Buchanan from Edinburgh against Glasgow's defending title-holder Jim Watt—an all Scottish match-up. Going into the contest, Buchanan was by far the more experienced fighter, having a record of forty-five victories against two defeats, having met a host of world-class fighters. Watt entered the fray with a tally of fifteen wins and two defeats; as good as he was, it was notable that he had not met the same calibre of fighter during his career that Buchanan had. This was a factor that was more than relevant and could well tell against Watt during the course of the championship contest. Watt, however, acquitted himself well and hence gave indications of his world-class potential by giving Buchanan a difficult night. Jim lost a fifteen round points decision, which was by no means a disgrace against one of the top lightweights in the world. On this occasion, Ken won the Lonsdale Belt outright, having first won the domestic crown on 19 February 1968 by knocking out holder Maurice Cullen in round eleven of fifteen at the Hilton Hotel in Mayfair, London. Buchanan made a first defence against Brian Hudson on 12 May 1970 at the Empire Pool in London. Buchanan had kept hold of his title by knocking out Hudson in round five of a proposed fifteen-round contest. Ken later relinquished the British crown. Watt hence regrouped from the loss to Buchanan not only to regain the British championship but to go on to capture the European and WBC world lightweight titles in future fights.

American Carol Polis made history when she became the first female to be appointed as a judge to officiate at professional boxing matches. Carol's first assignment took place on 19 February 1973 at the Spectrum in Philadelphia, Pennsylvania, judging the contest between Earnie Shavers and Jimmy Young. The contest concluded in favour of Shavers when he stopped Young in three rounds of a scheduled ten.

On 12 March 1973, Japan's Kuniaki Shibata stepped up to challenge Philippines-born Ben Villaflor for the WBA super-featherweight title at the Honolulu International Center in Hawaii. At the end of the fifteen-round battle, Shibata was awarded the points decision and became the new champion. By winning this title, Shibata became the first Japanese fighter

Jim Watt may have lost his British lightweight title to Ken Buchanan in 1973 but showed in defeat that he had the potential to go far in the future. (*Les Clark*)

to win a world title in two weight divisions when boxing abroad. The first world championship win away from home on foreign shores took place on 11 December 1970 when Shibata took to the ring at the Auditorio Municipal, Tijuana. Shibata had the difficult task of taking on the home fighter Vicente Saldivar, who was making the first defence in his second as reign as WBC world featherweight crown. Shibata emerged victorious when Saldivar retired in round twelve of a contest scheduled for fifteen.

Chris Finnegan had to fight off a determined attack from challenger Roy John to retain his British and Commonwealth light-heavyweight titles at the Empire Pool on 13 March 1973. The contest went the full fifteen rounds, with the points decision going to the champion. John was the second Welshman to be defeated by Finnegan in a championship clash. Finnegan had won the respective titles from the then champion Eddie Avoth on 24 January 1971 at the Grosvenor House (World Sporting Club) in Mayfair, London, by a fifteen-round stoppage.

Ken Norton was without question a fine fighter who more than proved his worth among the top-flight-heavyweights during his career. Norton cemented his status when he became just the second man in the division

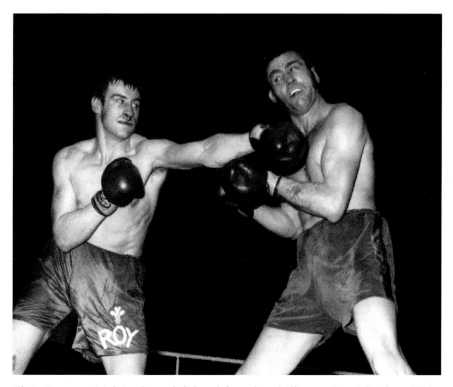

Chris Finnegan (right) takes a left hand from his challenger Roy John from Wales when defending his British light-heavyweight crown in 1973. (*Derek Rowe*)

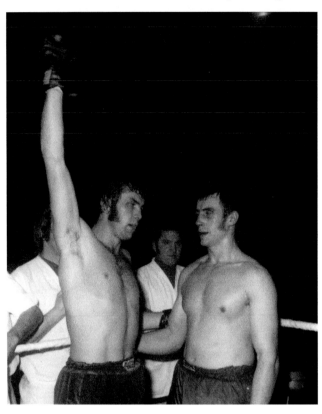

At the end of their fifteen-round encounter, Chris Finnegan retained his British light-heavyweight title by outpointing Roy John over fifteen rounds. (*Derek Rowe*)

to defeat Muhammad Ali in the professional ranks. Then a former world heavyweight champion, Ali lost his NABF heavyweight title, which he was then defending on points over twelve rounds to Norton on 31 March 1973 at the Sports Arena, San Diego, California. However, Norton also holds a further unique record: that of being the only man to hold a version of the world heavyweight crown without ever winning a title bout. On 26 March 1974, Ken challenged George Foreman for the undisputed title and was duly stopped in round two of fifteen at the El Poliedro in Caracas, Venezuela. The second challenge came on 28 September 1976 at the Yankee Stadium in New York when Norton met defending champion Muhammad Ali and hence lost a fifteen-round points decision.

Then on 5 November 1977, Ken met Jimmy Young in a final eliminator at Caesars Palace in Las Vegas, Nevada, and won a fifteen-round points decision. However, the then champion Leon Spinks defended his title against Muhammad Ali (whom he had previously beaten for the championship) rather than Norton. So the WBC stripped their version of the title from Spinks and made Norton their new champion. However, the fates were not on Ken's side since he lost the crown in his first defence at

Caesars Palace Sports Pavilion, Las Vegas, when outpointed over fifteen rounds by Larry Holmes in Las Vegas on 9 June 1978.

A much-anticipated match took place on 22 May 1973 when Chris Finnegan and John Conteh crossed swords at the Empire Pool. It was a triple championship affair with Finnegan, a former holder of the European crown putting his British and Commonwealth light-heavyweight titles on the line. Conteh (the reigning European champion) was also putting his crown at stake in the contest. At the end of the exciting fifteen-round bout in which both fighters gave their best, Conteh emerged the winner when he took a points decision. This was the first time since 16 October 1951 (when then champion Don Cockell knocked out Albert Finch in round seven of a scheduled fifteen (the contest also for Cockell's British crown) at the Harringay Arena, London) that two British fighters had fought each other for a European title in this division.

Larry Paul met former British welterweight champion Bobby Arthur for the inaugural British super-welterweight crown at the Civic Hall in Wolverhampton, West Midlands, on 25 September 1973. Paul was going into the bout undefeated in just eight bouts while Arthur was no stranger to the 'punch for pay' ranks, having competed on thirty-one occasions

John Conteh (left) and Chris Finnegan fought in 1973 for the British, European, and Commonwealth light-heavyweight titles. (*Derek Rowe*)

(winning twenty-three times with eight losses). The question that had to be asked was whether Arthur knew a little too much for his opponent, who obviously lacked his experience. Paul answered that question empathically on the night, proving to be a talented and confident performer, overcoming any shortcomings his lack of experience may have held. It also transpired that Paul was the stronger puncher of the two and became the first title-holder in the division when he knocked out Arthur in the tenth round of a contest scheduled for fifteen.

Alan Minter was a boxer who went on to win the undisputed world, British European, and British middleweight titles. Along the way, Minter met and defeated a host of quality fighters on his journey to the top. However, there was one fighter during the early stages of his career who became a roadblock to his advancement in the professional ranks. That man was fellow Briton Jan Magdziarz, whom Minter met on three occasions with disastrous results. The pair first met on 30 October 1973 at the Royal Albert Hall in Kensington in a contest set for eight rounds. Minter was boxing well but was halted in the third round when he sustained a cut right eye, giving his opponent the victory. The ending was very inconclusive so the two met again on 11 December 1973, the venue being the former battleground, the Royal Albert Hall. The contest was set for eight rounds but once more it failed to run its full course when Minter retired in round six due to a badly cut eye. On 29 October 1974, the two men for the third time crossed gloves at the Royal Albert Hall in a contest that was an eliminator for the British middleweight championship. This time, Minter looked set to put the record straight and defeat his foe in fine style, except this was not a case of third time lucky. Both boxers were disqualified in round four of ten for not giving their best. This would be the last time that the two would meet for pay in the ring as no fourth meeting ever took place. Minter reached the very top of his professional career, but Magdziarz was one fighter he just could not add to his victory list.

It was an interesting contest on 11 February 1974 at the Hilton Hotel Mayfair in London when British middleweight title-holder Bunny Sterling put his championship on the line against challenger Kevin Finnegan. It was a difficult one to call as both were talented boxers, but Sterling appeared to have all the ring smarts to turn back his opponent and keep the crown. Finnegan, however, really rose to the occasion and shocked Sterling, revealing his skills by outpointing him over fifteen rounds to claim the championship. In turn, Finnegan showed that he was a fighter with promise who could well go beyond domestic honours in the fullness of time.

Guts Ishimatsu became the first Japanese boxer to win a version of the world lightweight title when he knocked out defending WBC champion Rodolfo Gonzalez of Mexico in round eight of fifteen. The contest took

In three contests, Alan Minter (right) was not able to get past opponent Jan Magdziarz. (*Derek Rowe*)

Bunny Sterling (left) ducks under a right hand from Kevin Finnegan. (*Derek Rowe*)

Kevin Finnegan (left)
shocked Bunny Sterling
in 1974, taking his
British middleweight
title. (*Derek Rowe*)

place on 11 April 1974 at the Nihon University Auditorium in Tokyo, Japan. Ishimatsu had worked hard to acquire this championship, which had, at times, looked well beyond his reach—a fact proven with this victory over Gonzalez, this being his third endeavour to win the crown. The Japanese had his first crack at the undisputed title on 6 June 1970 against the reigning champion Ismael Laguna at the Gimnasio Nuevo, Panama City. An excellent boxer, Laguna had home advantage in his title defence and did not disappoint his fans. In a contest scheduled for fifteen rounds, Laguna stopped his challenger in round thirteen. Once again, in his second shot at the lightweight title, Ishimatsu had to travel to Panama. At the same venue where he previously faced Laguna, the Japanese challenger had to face the awesome WBA king Roberto Duran; few, if any, gave Ishimatsu any chance of victory. In the scheduled fifteen round championship fight, the Japanese challenger bravely lasted until round ten before the heavy-handed Duran stopped him.

A new European super-featherweight champion was crowned on 7 May 1974 when defending title-holder Lothar Abend of Germany was stopped in round three of fifteen by challenger Svein Erik Paulsen at the Jordal Amfi in Oslo, Norway. By gaining victory in this contest, Paulsen became the first professional boxer from Norway to win a European title.

When two British boxers in the shape of John H. Stracey (welterweight) and Kevin Finnegan (middleweight) travelled to France on 27 May 1974 to challenge for European titles in their own respective weight divisions, few gave them a chance of succeeding in their quest against quality champions defending on home turf. It was often hard enough to win one European title, especially when challenging away from home in the champion's own backyard, but two in one night on the same card hardly likely. However, at the Stade Roland Garros in Paris, the pair pulled off magnificent victories to claim the titles against fighters who were proven world-class operators. Stracey fought well to stop Roger Menetrey, who was making the sixth defence of the title in round eight of fifteen. Menetrey had taken the European crown from Stracey's stablemate Ralph Charles on 4 June 1971 by a seven-round knockout in a contest scheduled for fifteen at the Ice Stadium in Geneva, Switzerland. Finnegan too put on a superb display of boxing to outpoint Jean Claude Bouttier over fifteen rounds. Bouttier was making a first defence in his second reign as champion. The victories gave British boxing a great boost on the night and confirmed that both by Stracey and Finnegan belonged in the top ten rankings in the world.

Madison Square Garden on 17 June 1974 saw the great former legendary world heavyweight champion Joe Louis duck between the ropes once again, not of course in the role of fighter but in the capacity of referee. The bout he was handling was the encounter between former world heavyweight king Joe Frazier and Jerry Quarry; it was set for the duration of ten rounds. A contest between the two hard-punching fighters came to a finish in the fifth round when Louis stepped in to stop the hard-hitting contest, giving Frazier the victory.

American heavyweight Jack O'Halloran had his last professional contest on 16 August 1974 at the Coliseum in San Diego, California. O'Halloran left the ring that night after being knocked out in round six of ten by fellow countryman Howard Smith. During his time in the paid ranks, O'Halloran comprised a record of fifty-seven bouts (winning thirty-four, losing twenty-one, and drawing two). Jack was no stranger to British fans, having fought in the UK on four occasions. On 15 April 1969, he lost an eight-round points decision to future British, European, and Commonwealth heavyweight champion Joe Bugner at the Royal Albert Hall in Kensington. On his second visit, O'Halloran outpointed Carl Gizzi over ten rounds at the World Sporting Club in Mayfair on 7 July 1969. Danny McAlinden, the future British and Commonwealth heavyweight king, was defeated by the American on points over eight rounds on 6 July 1970 at Grosvenor House in Mayfair. It started to look as if O'Halloran was proving to be a risky opponent for British opponents to take on but former British heavyweight champion Jack Bodell turned the tide when

Above: Roger Menetrey (left) lost his European welterweight crown to John H. Stracey in 1974. (*Derek Rowe*)

Below: John H. Stracey with the newly won European welterweight title belt, adding to his already held Lonsdale Belt, which he is wearing around his waist. (*Derek Rowe*)

On the same night in 1974, Kevin Finnegan gave the UK a great double victory when he won the European middleweight title, defeating holder Jean-Claude Bouttier. (*Derek Rowe*)

in a ten-round contest staged at the Civic Hall in Wolverhampton in the West Midlands on 24 February 1971, he knocked the American out in the fourth session. After retiring from the sport, Jack turned his hand to acting and secured roles in two *Superman* films, *Farewell, My Lovely*, and *Dragnet*.

Liverpool's John Conteh had his night of glory when he outpointed Argentina's Jorge Ahumada over fifteen rounds at the Empire Pool, Wembley, London, on 1 October 1974 to capture the vacant WBC world light-heavyweight championship. This was not an easy assignment for Conteh since the man from Argentina had no quit in him and proved to be one tough *hombre* who pushed the Briton all the way. Conteh could not relax for one moment against this dangerous opponent. Ahumada had not made the trip to Britain just to be a victim for the British fighter; he arrived with the firm intention of adding the championship to his name when the proceedings came to its conclusion.

Ahumada had made a previous challenge for the undisputed title at the University Arena in Albuquerque, New Mexico, on 17 June 1974. Ahumada did well in his bid but failed to take the title when the fight was deemed to be a fifteen-round draw against the reigning champion Bob

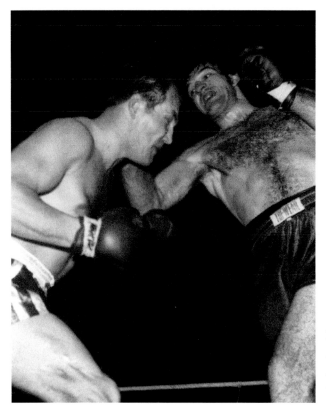

Jack Bodell (left) set
to repel the attack of
American opponent
Jack O'Halloran
in their 1971 bout.
(*Derek Rowe*)

Foster of America. Foster was a hard-punching fighter who was fated to be ranked among the greats of the division; however, to be truthful, he was not the force he once was when facing Ahumada. Such as it is with all fighters, time and hard-fought battles were beginning to catch up with him. Many felt Ahumada deserved another shot at Foster but it was not forthcoming.

Soon after the defence against the Argentinian fighter, Foster announced his retirement, leaving both the WBC and WBA titles vacant. Conteh, a man who many pundits felt had the talent to go far in the sport, was then matched against Ahumada and made the most of his opportunity boxing superbly to fill the WBC vacancy. The two fighters picked to fill the WBA void was another Argentinian Victor Galindez and American Len Hutchins. At the Estadio Luna Park, Buenos Aires, Distrito Federal in Argentina on 7 December 1974, Galindez claimed the crown when Hutchins retired in the twelfth session of a fifteen-round scheduled contest. It appeared that it would be just a matter of time before Conteh met Galindez in a unification contest; however, such a meeting failed to take place, though it would have surely been a fight to remember. When

Conteh defeated Ahumada, he became the first British fighter to hold a major version of this championship since Freddie Mills, who held the undisputed crown from 1948–1950.

If anyone could do the impossible and beat the odds, it had to be Muhammad Ali; time and time again, he continued to amaze the experts and revealed that he was not a man to bet against in the boxing arena. In George Foreman, Ali was up against an undefeated fighter who had won all his forty bouts; a man who was a proven puncher who had stopped or knocked out thirty-seven opponents, he looked as if he could punch holes in a wall—such was his power at the time. He was a fighter who instilled fear in his opponents. However, once again, with a record of forty-six bouts (winning forty-four, thirty-one inside the scheduled distance with two defeats), Ali showed in no uncertain manner why he was one of the true greats in boxing. Putting in an exceptional display, Ali became just the second man in the professional ranks to regain the world heavyweight championship. At the Stade du 20 Mai Kinshasa, Democratic Republic of Congo, on 30 October 1974 in a hard-fought contest, Ali prevailed against the defending title-holder. Foreman gave his all in his efforts to knock out his challenge and hence keep the championship but he had no answer to the puzzle, which stood in front of him and thus surrendered the crown when Ali knocked him out in round eight of a bout scheduled for fifteen.

Bunny Johnson (born in Jamaica but based in London) stepped into the battle zone at Grosvenor House in London on 13 January 1975. He was to challenge Ireland's reigning champion Danny McAlinden for the British and Commonwealth heavyweight titles. Up to that moment in time, no black fighter had held the domestic championship in the division. That situation was about to change in no uncertain way when in round nine of fifteen, Johnson knocked out McAlinden to claim the title. Johnson also captured the Commonwealth title, which was also on the line.

On 9 February 1975, Daniel Trioulaire of France won the European bantamweight crown when he stopped Ghana-born but French resident Bob Allotey in round nine of a fifteen round contest. The bout took place at the Rouen, Seine-Maritime in France. After this victory, Trioulaire went on to become the first holder of a European bantamweight title to retain his title with three consecutive draws. The first defence of the title was against England's Dave Needham on 11 April 1975 at Barentin in Seine-Maritime, France. At the end of the fifteen-round contest, the points were even so the Frenchman retained the title. The second defence came against Ireland's Paddy Maguire on 16 January 1976. Once again, Trioulaire had home ground advantage with the fight being staged at the Gymnase de la Sardagne Cluses in Haute-Savoie, France. Once again, the contest ended in a fifteen-round draw. For his next defence, Troulaire ventured to Spain to meet challenger Fernando Bernardez on 7 April 1976. The spectators at the Vigo Galicia witnessed the contest go the full fifteen rounds and at the conclusion of the championship encounter, a draw was given. Everything eventually comes to an end; that also applies to drawn results. On 14 August 1976, the title left France when at the Ospedaletti, Liguria in Italy, home fighter Salvatore Fabrizio took the championship with a fifteen-round points decision.

Ken Buchanan, the former undisputed world lightweight champion, attempted to once again hold a world crown when he challenged the reigning WBC lightweight king Guts Ishimatsu of Japan. The task was not going to be easy for the Scot that was obvious from the start. The odds were stacked against him. However, it has to be said that when comparing their respective fight records, Ken had the better résumé—not only meeting but beating better opposition than the champion had during his time in the ring. Yet one must face the truth in such matters and the truth was Ken was not the fighter he once was. He was still an exceptional boxer who was more than capable of beating a number of top-ranked fighters but he had peaked somewhat. Had Buchanan fought Ishimatsu while still in his pomp, he would have been a firm favourite to win the title. Ken had to travel to the champion's own backyard on 27 February 1975 to do battle in a contest that took place at the Metropolitan Gym in Tokyo. After fifteen rounds of boxing, the title remained in Japan when Ishimatsu was given the points decision. This was the fifth and last time that Buchanan was to contest a world championship. Amazingly, Ken did not have one of his world fights in the UK. He first won the title WBA version on 26 September 1970, outpointing Panama's Ismael Laguna over fifteen rounds at the Hiram Brithorn Stadium, San Juan in Puerto Rico. A first defence followed on 12 February 1971 at the Sports Arena Los Angeles in California against American Ruben Navarro; this bout was not only for the WBA but also for the vacant WBC version of the title the Scot won the contest with a fifteen-round points decision. Next up was a return with Ismael Laguna at Madison Square Garden in New York for the WBA version of the crown on 13 September 1971 with a fifteen-round points victory for the Scot (Buchanan had been stripped of his WBC title). Then it was back to Madison Square Garden on 26 June 1972 where Ken was stopped in round thirteen of fifteen for the WBA championship by Panama's Roberto Duran. It was a great shame that Ken did not have the comfort of fighting for a world title on his own turf during his career.

The first world contest for the WBC world light-flyweight crown took place on 4 April 1975 between Franco Udella of Italy and Mexico's Valentin Martinez at the San Siro Stadium in Milan, Italy. Udella emerged victorious, gaining a twelve-round disqualification victory over his opponent. The contest was scheduled for fifteen rounds.

Ken Buchanan failed to regain the WBC world lightweight crown in 1975 when he had to travel to Japan to challenge the champion. (*Derek Rowe*)

Australian Billy Moeller became the first man to be crowned the Commonwealth super-featherweight champion. Moeller achieved this feat on 13 May 1975 at the Saint Mary's Band Club in Sydney, Australia. Moeller won the title when he outpointed Scottish-born Australian resident Jimmy Bell over fifteen rounds in the inaugural contest.

Saensak Muangsurin won a world championship in the fewest number of fights on 15 July 1975; this happened when defending WBC world super-lightweight champion Perico Fernandez of Spain was knocked out in round eight in a bout set for fifteen at the Hua Mark, Indoor Stadium in Bangkok in Thailand. Home fighter Muangsurin was amazingly on just his third contest in the paid ranks.

Jaime Rios of Panama became the first holder of the WBA version of the world light-flyweight title on 23 August 1975. Rios claimed the inaugural crown with a competitive fifteen-round points decision against Venezuela opponent Rigoberto Marcano at the Gimnasio Nuevo Panama in Panama City.

On 13 September 1975, Luis Estaba delighted his home fans when he won the vacant WBC world light-flyweight championship by knocking out opponent Rafael Lovera of Paraguay in round four of fifteen at the Nuevo Circo Bullring in Caracas, Venezuela. While Lovera may not have been successful in his bid for the title he hence gained a degree of attention by becoming the first fighter to challenge for a world championship at this poundage in his very first professional contest.

David Kotey became the first boxer from Ghana to win a world title in the professional ranks on 20 September 1975 when he outpointed the defending champion Ruben Olivares of Mexico over fifteen rounds to win the WBC world featherweight crown. This event took place at the Forum Inglewood in California. Kotey held on to the title until his third defence where he surrendered his crown when losing a fifteen-round points decision to American challenger Danny Lopez at the Accra Sports Stadium in Ghana on 6 November 1976. Kotey attempted to regain the championship in a return contest with Lopez on 15 February 1978 but failed in his bid when stopped in round six of a scheduled fifteen-round encounter, the venue being the Hilton Hotel in Las Vegas Nevada.

John H. Stracey travelled to the Monumental Plaza de Toros in Mexico City on 6 December 1975 to challenge Cuban-born Mexican Jose Napoles for the WBC world welterweight championship. Stracey was a talented boxer who during his career had won the British and European titles. Yet the chances of John coming back to the UK with the crown looked slim as he was crossing gloves with an outstanding title-holder who looked as if his name was going to be added to the list of greats in the division. The Briton had met good fighters during his career but had not faced such a formidable opponent in the professional ring as the defending title-holder. The other problem John had to overcome was the country's high altitude, which gave many visiting fighters difficulty and should the encounter scheduled for fifteen go into the later rounds, this too would prove to be a telling factor. When the fight got underway, John made a bad start, taking a count in the first round that indicated that he may bow out of the contest early. However, with full belief in his ability, the Briton gritted his teeth to fight back and make foolish the predictions of a Stracey loss. The challenger secured his win when he defeated the champion in impressive style, stopping him in round six to provide one of the shocks of the year. In victory, Stracey became the first English fighter to win a world title in this division since Ted Kid Lewis, who reigned from 1915–1916 and 1917–1919.

Pat Thomas achieved a first on 15 December 1975 when at the Manor Place Baths, Walworth, London, he won the vacant British welterweight championship by knocking out former British super-lightweight king

John H. Stracey gave UK
boxing a tremendous boost
when he did the unexpected
and won the WBC world
welterweight title in Mexico in
1975. (*Derek Rowe*)

Pat McCormack of Ireland in round thirteen in a contest set for fifteen.
Thomas considered a Welsh fighter was actually born in Saint Kitts and
Nevis and hence became the first immigrant to win this title.

On 13 January 1976, Marvin Hagler had his undefeated record taken
from him in his twenty-seventh paid contest (this included one draw) at
the Spectrum, Philadelphia. The opponent who put a dent in Hagler's near
perfect record was fellow American Bobby Watts, who had a résumé of
twenty-seven wins, three defeats, and one draw. Watts, who at the time
was a decent fighter, took a ten-round points decision over Hagler. A return
contest looked to be an obvious match to be made and indeed materialised
on 20 April 1980. Hagler took his revenge at the Cumberland County
Civic Center, Portland, when in a contest scheduled for ten rounds, he
stopped Watts in the second stanza.

Wilfred Benitez captured the WBA world super-lightweight crown on 6
March 1976 when he outpointed defending champion Antonio Cervantes
of Columbia over fifteen rounds in front of his own countrymen at the
Hiram Bithorn Stadium in San Juan, Puerto Rico. On this occasion, youth
had its day since Benitez (at the age of seventeen years, five months, and

twenty-three days) created fistic history by becoming the youngest man at the time to win a world championship in the professional ranks.

Panama's Rigoberto Riasco became the first holder of the WBC world super-bantamweight title on 3 April 1976 when he defeated opponent Waruinge Nakayama of Kenya, who retired in round eight of a scheduled fifteen. The contest took place at the Gimnasio Nuevo Panama, Panama City.

On 20 April 1976, Maurice Hope retained his British super-welterweight title by stopping his challenger Tony Poole in round twelve of a contest set for fifteen at York Hall in Bethnal Green, London. In so doing, Hope became the first man in the division to win a Lonsdale Belt outright. In this bout, Hope also captured the vacant Commonwealth title, which was at stake. Hope had won the British championship on 5 November 1974 when at the Civic Hall in Wolverhampton, he took the crown from the defending title-holder Larry Paul by a knockout in round eight of a scheduled fifteen. The two met again on 30 September 1975, but once again, Paul met with defeat when at the Empire Pool, he was stopped in round four in a bout set for fifteen.

A family double was completed at the 1976 Olympic Games, which were staged in Montreal, Canada, when the Spinks brothers of America both won a gold medal in their respective weight divisions. Michael

From left to right: Jim Watt, Colin Hart (boxing journalist), and Maurice Hope, who became the first boxer to win the Lonsdale Belt outright in the super-welterweight division. (*Derek Rowe*)

won his medal at middleweight, stopping Rufat Riskiyev of the Soviet Union by way of a stoppage in round three. Leon won his medal at light-heavyweight, stopping his opponent Sixto Soria of Cuba in the third round.

On 1 October 1976, Maurice Hope became Britain's first European champion at super-welterweight when he stopped defending title-holder Vito Antuofermo of Italy in round fifteen at the Palazzetto dello Sport in Rome, Italy. Hope knew that he would be in for a hard night against a tough opponent but put on a fine exhibition of boxing in what was his first professional contest abroad. This was a better victory than first realised for Hope since Antuofermo recovered from this defeat and moved up a division and later won the world middleweight crown, outpointing Argentina's Hugo Pastor Corro over fifteen rounds at the Chapiteau de l' Espace, Fontvieille, Monaco, on 30 June 1979.

Dave (Boy) Green lived up to expectations when he punched his way to the vacant European super-lightweight title on 7 December 1976. Green entered the ring as the favourite to lift the championship. The Briton's opponent was Jean-Baptiste Piedvanche of France, who found the Fen Tiger too strong to handle and retired in round nine of fifteen. The contest, which took place at the Royal Albert Hall in London, saw Green become the first British boxer to win the European crown in this division.

It was not expected to be an easy outing for British middleweight champion Alan Minter at the Royal Albert Hall on 7 December 1976. He was to face American Sugar Ray Seales—a smooth operator who was clearly not a pushover; a win for Minter was not a foregone conclusion. Like Minter, Seales was ranked in the world ten and had every intention of returning home with a victory that would further boost his rating and enhance his chances of getting a crack at the world title. Seales had previously won thirty-one of his previous fights, losing two, and drawing one; like Minter, he was a southpaw. Seales was ready to rumble, ready to go to war; so too was Minter, making for an explosive cocktail. One of the interesting facts about the pairing of these two fighters was that both had competed at the 1972 Munch Olympic Games. Minter had claimed a bronze medal in the light middleweight division while Seales had secured a gold medal at light welterweight. After a competitive action-packed contest, Minter survived some rocky moments and showed true grit to topple his opponent and march towards a world title tilt, winning by a stoppage in round five of ten, taking his professional record to thirty-one fights, losing four with one no contest.

Wilfredo Gomez of Puerto Rico won the WBC version of the world super-bantamweight title on 21 May 1977 by knocking out defending champion Dong Kyun Yum of Korea in round twelve of fifteen at the

Above: Dave (Boy) Green (left), who became the first British holder of the European super-lightweight title in 1976, seen with Alan Minter, Maurice Hope, and Jim Watt. (*Derek Rowe*)

Left: Alan Minter engaged in a war with American opponent Sugar Ray Seales in 1976 at the Royal Albert Hall. (*Derek Rowe*)

Roberto Clemente Coliseum in San Juan, Puerto Rico. Gomez proved to be an outstanding champion who went on to make seventeen consecutive defences of the title—a record in the division at that time. Gomez made the last defence of the championship on 3 December 1982 against Lupe Pintor of Mexico at the Superdome, New Orleans, which resulted in a fourteen-round stoppage of fifteen for the champion. Gomez later relinquished the title to move up a division to featherweight.

Alan Minter (the reigning European middleweight champion and future world middleweight king) fought at the Stade Louis II in Fontvieille, Monaco, on 30 July 1977. Minter's opponent was the former world welterweight and middleweight champion Emile Griffith. Minter boxed his way to a ten-round points decision and in accomplishing this feat became the first British boxer to defeat Griffith. Previously, the fighter (who had been born in the Virgin Islands) had defeated Welshman Brian Curvis (the then British and Commonwealth welterweight champion) over fifteen rounds on 22 September 1964 at the Empire Pool. Griffith was defending his world welterweight crown and was a clear winner over his brave challenger who just could not get the better of the classy champion. Once again at the Empire Pool on 1 December 1964 in a ten-round non-title bout, Griffith stopped Dave Charnley (the British Lightweight champion and former European and Commonwealth king) in round nine. Harry Scott was the next Briton to experience the skills of Griffith in a scheduled ten-round bout at the Royal Albert Hall in London on 4 October 1965. Scott was defeated when he retired in round seven. While Griffith's is a good name on Minter's record, it was obvious during the course of the contest that the man whom the Briton beat on the night was just a pale shadow of the fighter he once was; he was way past his best and only going through the motions as time and tough fights had caught up to him. This proved to be Griffith's last professional contest.

On 29 September 1977, Muhammad Ali made the tenth defence in his second reign as world heavyweight champion at Madison Square Garden in New York, outpointing a dangerous challenger in the shape of hard-punching Earnie Shavers over fifteen rounds. On this night, history was made, not by Ali but by Eva Shain, who hence became the first woman to officiate as a judge at a world heavyweight championship contest.

Soo-Hwan Hong of South Korea became the first holder of the WBA world super-bantamweight title on 26 November 1977 at the Gimnasio Nuevo Panama, Panama City. Hong accomplished this feat by defeating home fighter Hector Carrasquilla by way of a knockout in round three of a bout scheduled for fifteen.

The hard-punching Charlie Magri was a man who breathed new life into the British flyweight division. This sad case of affairs was due to the

Alan Minter became
the first British fighter
to defeat former world
welterweight and
middleweight champion
Emile Griffith in 1977.
(*Derek Rowe*)

lack of fighters at the weight in Britain. In the past, the UK had produced many outstanding fighters at flyweight competitors who had won versions of the world championship. Magri was a real crowd-pleaser who really packed a punch and excited the fans with his exciting performances whenever he fought in the ring. This in turn brought a renewed and most welcomed interest to the weight division it really looked as if Magri could take the poundage back to the golden days of yesteryear. Charlie made a rapid rise to championship status. On 6 December 1977, he entered the square ring to contest the vacant British flyweight crown against opponent Dave Smith, who was undefeated in eight fights, having a record of seven wins and one draw at the Royal Albert Hall. Magri lived up to expectations and showed that the promise many pundits had in him was not misplaced in any way whatsoever when he took the honours, stopping his opponent in round seven of fifteen. Remarkably, this was just Magri's third professional contest.

Spain's Roberto Castanon stepped into the ring on 16 December 1977 to challenge fellow countryman Manuel Masso for the European featherweight crown. The venue for the contest was the Palacio de los Deportes, Barcelona. The championship bout was scheduled for fifteen rounds but failed to go that distance when Castanon won the crown, knocking out Masso in round eleven. Castanon went on to defend the title eleven times, creating at the time a record for the division. Castanon eventually relinquished the championship and moved up a weight division to super-featherweight.

On the surface, it looked like an easy defence for Muhammad Ali on 15 February 1978 when he put his world heavyweight crown on the line against Leon Spinks, a man who was vastly inexperienced in the professional ranks, having taken part in just seven bouts prior to his meeting with the champion. It looked as if Spinks was on his way to a defeat, possibly a stoppage well inside the distance. A win was unthinkable; experts were not sure how a mere novice in professional terms could possibly beat a master of the boxing ring with so few professional fights behind him. It seemed Spinks was on his way to a painful boxing lesson. However, after fifteen rounds at the Hilton Hotel in Las Vegas, challenger Spinks shocked the boxing world when he outpointed Ali and became champion in just his eighth bout. In so doing, he created at the time a record of having won the world heavyweight crown with the fewest contests.

Jim Watt looked to be on a tough assignment on 17 February 1978 when he ducked under the ropes at the Palacio de los Deportes in Madrid to defend his European title against Spanish challenger Perico Fernandez. Fernandez was not an easy man to overcome, having previously held the WBC world super-lightweight and European super-lightweight and lightweight championship. At that moment in time, no fighter from the UK had won a European title contest in Spain. Alan Rudkin challenged Mimoun Ben Ali for the European bantamweight title on 27 April 1967, losing a fifteen-round points decision. Ken Buchanan ventured fourth on 29 January 1970 to contest the vacant European lightweight title against Miguel Velazquez, falling short when on the wrong side of a fifteen-round points decision. Rudkin, then the defending European bantamweight king, tasted defeated for a second time on Spanish soil on 10 August 1971 against Agustin Senin when outpointed over the duration of fifteen rounds. Jack Bodell defended his European heavyweight championship against former holder Jose Manuel Urtain, but left the country without his crown when knocked out in round two of fifteen on 17 December 1971. Under the circumstances, many pundits were not very enthusiastic about Watt's chances of retaining his crown. At the start of the contest, the prospects of a win for the British fighter did indeed not look too good when he was floored for a count in the opening round. However, Watt overcame this setback and fought back earnestly. Hence on the night, Watt proved that he was a genuine world-class boxer, outpointing his vastly experienced opponent over fifteen rounds to remain king of Europe and earning the accolade of being the first fighter from Britain to win a European title bout in Spain.

After his shock defeat, a return with Leon Spinks was a must for Muhammad Ali in a contest that took place on 15 September 1978. The venue where the two met was the Superdome in New Orleans. This was an intriguing match, with the major question being whether Spinks could repeat his victory or if Ali would gain his revenge. The defeat by Spinks the first time could have been a fluke or a sign that Ali was nearing the end of his magnificent career in the ring. After fifteen rounds of boxing, Ali answered those two questions when he emerged victorious with a points win to become the first man in the history of boxing to twice regain the world heavyweight crown. Since the WBC had previously stripped their version of the title from Spinks due to his failure to defend the crown against their number one contender Ken Norton, it was just the WBA championship on the line in the contest with Ali. After this bout, Ali retired from boxing. Ali returned to the sport at a later date.

American Marvin Johnson made his mark in the light-heavyweight division by becoming the first fighter at the poundage to win a version of the world crown on three separate occasions. He first became a global champion on 2 December 1978. Johnson travelled to Italy to challenge Mate Parlov of Croatia for the WBC world light-heavyweight title. The venue was the Palazzo dello Sport in Marsala, Sicily. The bout was slated for

Jim Watt (left) seen with Colin Hart and Maurice Hope; he became the first Briton to win a European title fight in Spain during 1978. (*Derek Rowe*)

fifteen rounds but ended in a ten-round stoppage that saw the crown change hands and Johnson crowned the new king. On 22 April 1979, Johnson lost the championship in his first defence at the Market Square Arena in Indianapolis, Indiana, when stopped in the eighth session of a fifteen-round contest by fellow countryman Matthew Saad Muhammad. Before the year came to an end, Johnson had another chance to become a world champion when WBA holder Victor Galindez of Argentina put his crown on the line. At the Superdome, New Orleans, Johnson knocked out Galindez in round eleven of a scheduled fifteen. On 31 March 1980, Johnson faced fellow American Eddie Mustafa Muhammad at the Stokley Athletics Center in Knoxville, Tennesse in his first defence. Johnson once again found himself a former world champion when he was stopped in round eleven of fifteen by his challenger. On 9 February 1986, Johnson found himself challenging for the WBA version of the light-heavyweight championship at the Market Square Arena, Indianapolis. The crown was vacant but Johnson filled that vacancy when he stopped opponent Leslie Stewart of Trinidad and Tobago in round seven of a bout set for fifteen. Johnson made a successful defence against French fighter Jean Marie Emebe on 20 September 1986, once again the venue being Market Square, Indianpolis, winning by a stoppage in round thirteen of fifteen. In a return with Stewart on 23 May 1987 at the National Stadium in Port-of-Spain, Trinidad and Tobago, Johnson retired in round eight in a bout set for twelve. This was Johnson's last professional outing since soon after, he retired from the sport, having participated in forty-nine fights (winning forty-three and losing six).

Maurice Hope became Britain's first holder of the world super-welterweight title when he challenged holder Rocky Mattioli for the WBC version of the championship on 4 March 1979. Hope had it all to do, contesting the crown in the title-holder's country. The venue was the Teatro Ariston in Sanremo, Italy. The spectators were clearly on the side of the home fighter, but this did not help the champion's cause for Hope stopped Mattioli in the eighth round of fifteen.

Jim Watt of Scotland won the vacant WBC world lightweight crown on 17 April 1979 when he stopped Columbia's Alfredo Pitalua in round twelve of fifteen at the Kelvin Hall in Glasgow. The WBC title was up for grabs when Panama's Roberto Duran relinquished it to move to another weight division. The contest between Witt and Pitalua was the first world championship to be staged in Scotland since home fighter Jackie Patterson made a successful defence of his world flyweight title against England's Joe Curran. Patterson outpointed his challenger over fifteen rounds at Hampden Park, Glasgow, in a contest that took place on 10 July 1946. Also at stake in the contest was Patterson's British and Commonwealth flyweight title and European bantamweight crown.

Maurice Hope became the first UK holder of the world super-welterweight title when he won the WBC version in 1979. (*Derek Rowe*)

Charlie Magri pulled on the gloves on 1 May 1979 in his bid to become the first British fighter since Welshman Dai Dower to win the European flyweight title. Dower briefly held the crown in 1955. The challenge for Magri was the Italian Franco Udella, a former WBC world light-flyweight champion who was making the ninth defence of the European belt. Udella was an excellent fighter and would not give up the belt without making a fight of it. The battle between the two fighters took place at the Empire Pool in London. The confident Magri did not disappoint his many fans in attendance at the show; he fought well and claimed the title with a twelve-round points decision. Winning the championship against such an experienced fighter like Udella (who had participated in forty-two bouts: winning thirty-seven, losing four, with one no contest) spoke volumes for Magri, who was taking part in just his twelfth professional outing.

On 28 June 1979, Dave Boy Green (the European welterweight champion) paid a business visit to Denmark. Green was to defend his title against home fighter Joergen Hansen at the Randers Hallen. Despite

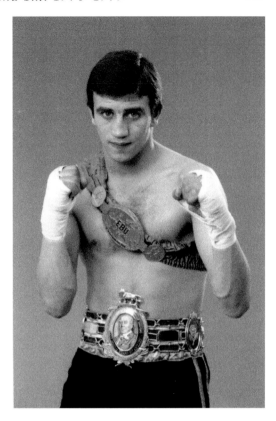

Charlie Magri won the European flyweight crown in 1979. (*Derek Rowe*)

fighting in his opponent's backyard, it was felt that the British fighter would leave the ring still as the reigning title-holder once the proceedings had come to its conclusion. It seemed a safe bet to say the contest would not go the full twelve rounds, with Green's hard-punching aggression being too much for the Dane to handle. As expected, the fight did not last the schedule distance but it was Hansen and not Green who punched his way to victory, scoring a knockout in round three to lift the crown. Not only did Hansen win the championship on this occasion, but he also became the first boxer to regain this title twice. Hansen first won the crown on 2 June 1977 when he knocked out holder Marco Scano of Italy in round five of a slated fifteen at the Randers Hallen Randers in Denmark.He became a former champion when in his first defence in Germany on 6 August 1977, he was disqualified against home fighter Joerg Eipel in round thirteen of a scheduled fifteen at the Deutschlandhalle in Charlottenburg, Berlin.

Another opportunity presented itself on 27 April 1978 for Hansen to become the king of the continent when Alain Marion of France stepped into the square ring at the Randers Hallen in Denmark to face the challenge of the former champion. Marion became an ex-title-holder when the Dane found the punches to dislodge him from his crown by way of a knockout in round six in a contest set for fifteen. The first defence by Hansen in his second reign against Austrian Joseph Pachler on 18 August 1978 proved a disaster when at the Stadthalle, Vienna, he was disqualified in round eight of the schedule fifteen-round encounter.

Pat Thomas became the first former British welterweight champion (he reigned from 1975 to 1976) to move up a division and capture the domestic crown at super-welterweight. Thomas accomplished this feat on 11 September 1979 at the Conference Centre in Wembley, London. The St Kitts-born Welshman challenged British title-holder Jimmy Batten of London for the crown and took the title by a stoppage in round nine in a bout scheduled for fifteen.

American Jimmy Young made his fourth and final appearance in a British ring on 4 December 1979, outpointing reigning British and Commonwealth heavyweight champion John L. Gardner over ten rounds. The contest, which took place at the Empire Pool, saw Young use his vast array of skills to get the better of his opponent. Young had found the UK a successful country in which to ply his wares, having had his first fight in Blighty on 22 October 1973 boxing an eight-round draw with Liverpool's Billy Aird at the Grosvenor House in Mayfair, London. Future British, European, and Commonwealth heavyweight king Richard Dunn found Young a difficult opponent to overcome when stopped in round eight of a contest scheduled for ten. This meeting took place on 18 February 1974 at the World Sporting Club in Mayfair. Les Stevens faired a little better than Dunn, lasting the full distance of ten rounds but losing the points decision. This contest took place on 22 April 1974, once again the venue being the World Sporting Club in Mayfair.

During his peak years, Young proved to be a class fighter even giving Muhammad Ali a hard night on 30 April 1976 when challenging for the world heavyweight title at the Capitol Centre in Landover, Maryland. Young lost a fifteen round points decision but gave the great Ali a headache or two along the way. Young's career came to a close on 13 August 1988 at Saint Joseph, Missouri, with him stopping fellow American Frank Lux in round ten. During his period in the paid ring, Young compiled a record of fifty-six fights (winning thirty-four, losing eighteen, with three drawn and one no contest).

Ken Buchanan failed in his attempt to regain the European lightweight crown at the Brondby Hallen in Denmark on 6 December 1979. The Scot was outpointed over twelve rounds by Northern Ireland's reigning title-holder, Charlie Nash. At this point, the former world lightweight champion was passed his best but was still a decent operator inside the ring. This was the first time that Buchanan had been defeated by a fellow fighter from the UK in the professional ranks.

The first contest for a world cruiserweight title took place on 8 December 1979 between two boxers who fought in the southpaw stance Marvin Camel of America and former WBC world light-heavyweight king Mate Parlov who during this meeting had home advantage. The WBC version of the championship was at stake at the Sportski Sports Centre in Split, Croatia. At the end of the hard-fought fifteen-round contest, the ringside judges were unable to find a clear winner and the bout was declared a draw. The two fighters met again, this time at Caesars Palace, Las Vegas on 31 March 1980; on this occasion, the division, found its first world champion when Camel was given the decision on points after fifteen rounds.

7

Round Seven: 1980–1989

Rafael Orono had the advantage of boxing on home ground when he brought the vacant WBC world super-flyweight title to Venezuela on 2 February 1980. Orono outpointed opponent Seung-Hoon Lee of South Korea over fifteen rounds at the Nuevo Circo, Caracas. This was the first world championship contest to be staged in this weight division.

Alan Minter won the world middleweight championship on 16 March 1980, outpointing Italian born title-holder Vito Antuofermo over fifteen rounds at Caesars Palace, Las Vegas. On acquiring the title, Minter became the first English-born boxer to win this championship on American soil since Bob Fitzsimmons, who claimed the title on 14 January 1891 when knocking out holder Irish Nonpareil Jack Dempsey in round thirteen in a fight to the finish at the Olympic Club, New Orleans. Fitzsimmons made a first successful defence on the knocking out New Zealand's Dan Creedon in round two in a bout scheduled for twenty-five at the same venue. Fitzsimmons later relinquished the middleweight crown to concentrate his efforts in the heavyweight division.

Teofilo Stevenson of Cuba became the second man to win three consecutive Olympic gold medals when at the 1980 Games, which were staged in Moscow; he outpointed opponent Piotz Zaev of the Soviet Union to take the honour. Stevenson had won his first medal in Munich in 1972 where he won gold by a walkover when opponent Ion Alexe of Romania was unable to compete due to injury. Then in Montreal, 1976, Stevenson took his second gold medal when he stopped Mircea Simon of Romania in the third round. All medals were won at heavyweight.

On 10 September 1980, Kevin Finnegan defended his European middleweight crown against Italian Matteo Salvemini losing a twelve-

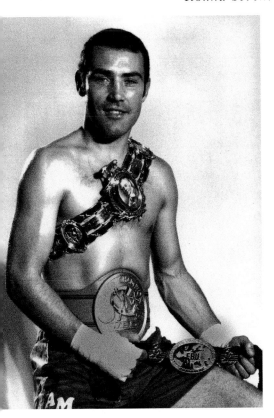

Alan Minter travelled to the USA in 1980 and captured the undisputed world middleweight championship. (*Derek Rowe*)

round points decision at the Teatro Ariston in Sanremo, Italy. The contest was the last for Finnegan, who bowed out of the sport with a résumé of forty-seven bouts (winning thirty-five, losing eleven, and drawing one). During his career, Kevin held the British middleweight title on three separate occasions and the European crown twice. Finnegan even made history with his older brother Chris Finnegan (light-heavyweight) as Chris and Kevin became the first brothers to win a Lonsdale Belt outright.

On 27 September 1980, boxing witnessed the crowning of a new world middleweight champion and a future great at Wembley Arena in London. American Marvin Hagler challenged Britain's Alan Minter, who was making the second defence of his title. The contest was explosive and short-lived between the two warring southpaws who went for it from the very start of the opening bell with serious intentions. It was clear that the contest was not going to last the scheduled distance of fifteen rounds; someone was going to be halted albeit by a knockout or stoppage. This was Hagler's second challenge for the title; his first crack at the championship took place on 30

Above left: Chris Finnegan. (*Derek Rowe*)

Above right: Kevin Finnegan. Along with Chris, they were the first brothers to each win a Lonsdale Belt outright. (*Derek Rowe*)

November 1979 against Vito Antuofermo (the man Minter took the world crown from). Hagler entered the ring on the night at Caesars Palace, Las Vegas, and fought the full fifteen rounds, feeling confident at the finish that the title was his and felt aggrieved when a draw decision was rendered. Hagler felt that he would right a wrong and this time take the championship. This he did in determined fashion when the title changed hands with Hagler stopping Minter in three ferocious, blood-splatted rounds. It was, however, a bad night for British boxing in more ways than one when a number of spectators who appeared to be racially motivated caused a riot, throwing bottles and various other objects into the ring. The new champion was quickly rushed to his dressing room for his own safety, hence spoiling his night of glory and what should have been a joyful occasion.

Few may not have realised it when watching the actual contest but reigning European champion and future WBC world flyweight title-holder

Alan Minter lost his world
middleweight title to Marvin
Hagler in 1980.
(*Derek Rowe*)

Charlie Magri recorded one of his best victories on 8 December 1980. Magri outscored Argentina's Santos Laciar over ten rounds in a hard-fought contest that took place at the Royal Albert Hall in London. Magri had to dig down deep and was made to fight every inch of the way to secure victory over his opponent in a crowd-pleasing encounter. Laciar was no ordinary fighter; he was a man who had championship quality written all over him and would later go on to prove his class in no uncertain way by capturing both the WBA world flyweight and WBC world super-flyweight titles at a future date.

It was one rugged battle at the Civic Auditorium in Stockton, California, on 8 March 1981 when champion and challenger went head-to-head with no quarter given. The WBC super-featherweight champion Rafael Limon of Mexico was one tough cookie, but the UK's Cornelius Boza-Edwards was equal to the task and took a hard but deserved fifteen-round points decision. In taking the win, Boza-Edwards became the first British fighter to win a world title belt in this division. Boza-Edwards was born in Uganda but was representing the UK.

Alexis Arguello became the first boxer from Nicaragua to win a world championship in three weight divisions when he came to the UK on 20 June 1981. At the Empire Pool, Wembley, Arguello outpointed defending WBC world lightweight champion Jim Watt over fifteen enthralling rounds to take the crown. Watt may have lost his title, but he fought with a champion's pride and could take some consolation by knowing that he at least lost to someone a little special. Prior to this encounter, Arguello had held the WBA featherweight and WBC super-featherweight titles.

A win for Barry McGuigan was very much expected when he stepped into the square ring on 3 August 1981 at the Corn Exchange in Brighton, Sussex. McGuigan, undefeated in two bouts, was felt to be too good for opponent Peter Eubank, who had boxed on seven occasions, winning three and losing four of his bouts. A surprise took place when Eubank outpointed McGuigan over eight rounds. A return bout between the two was natural and McGuigan knew he had to avenge the defeat and put the record straight. The two fighters took to the ring once more to do battle on 8 December 1981 at the Ulster Hall in Belfast, Northern Ireland. In front of his vocal fans, McGuigan had no intentions of letting the fight go to the scorecards on this occasion and defeated Eubank in the eighth and last round of their encounter. Peter Eubank was the brother of Chris Eubank, the future WBO world middleweight and super-middleweight king.

Nothing can be taken for granted in life—a fact which we are all aware of. This fact also applies to fight fans who, when seeing their favourite boxer mow down all the opponents he had previously confronted, feel this trend will surely continue. On 13 October 1981, at the Royal Albert Hall in London, Charlie Magri (who was undefeated in twenty-three professional fights) looked on course for a world title challenge; in fact, it looked only a matter of time before he went for global honours—he was perhaps one or two bouts away from such a prestigious occasion. So when Magri stepped in with Mexican Juan Diaz (who was not in any way special, with a record of thirty-nine bouts: winning twenty-one, losing sixteen, and drawing two), a win for the Briton seemed assured. It certainly seemed the bout would not go the full ten rounds. It was, in truth, a routine fight for Charlie—a marking time affair, keeping him busy and punch-sharp. True enough, the fight did not go the full ten rounds, but the result was not the expected one—far from it. Diaz produced a staggering shock to knock out Charlie in round six to set back any grand plans that may have been in the pipeline for him at the time.

A contest that took place on 28 November 1981 for the European super-welterweight title became the fastest ending contest for the championship in the division at that time. The defending title-holder Luigi Minchillo put his crown on the line against French challenger Claude Martin at the Rennes in Ille-et-Vilaine, France. Minchillo ensured that he would be taking the title back home to Italy with him when he knocked out Martin in a recorded fifteen seconds of the first round.

Ken Buchanan participated in his last professional contest on 25 January 1982 when outpointed by George Feeney over eight rounds at the National Sporting Club in Piccadilly, London. The Scot had an outstanding career and is considered by many experts to be one of the best fighters to emerge from the UK. Buchanan more than excelled in the ring, having won the undisputed world lightweight title, the British crown (winning a Lonsdale Belt outright), and the European crown. Buchanan fought a number of top-rated men, seven of whom held a version of the world title at one time or another during their time in the ring; these included men like Miguel Velazquez (WBC super-lightweight), Ismael Laguna (undisputed lightweight; a fighter he fought on two occasions), Carlos Hernandez (undisputed super-lightweight), Roberto Duran (undisputed lightweight WBC welterweight WBA super-welterweight and WBC middleweight), Carlos Ortiz (undisputed super-lightweight and lightweight), Jim Watt (WBC lightweight), and Guts Ishimatsu (WBC lightweight). Buchanan comprised a record of sixty-nine fights (winning sixty-one and losing eight); he was awarded an MBE to add to his many honours.

Cornelius Boza-Edwards brought the European super-featherweight championship to the UK for the first time on 17 March 1982 when at the Royal Albert Hall in London, where he claimed the crown. The defending title-holder, Carlos Hernandez of Spain, retired in round four of a scheduled twelve.

Miguel Canto brought his career to a close on 24 July 1982 at the Carte Clara Baseball Park in Merida, Mexico. A former WBC world flyweight champion, Canto was stopped in the ninth round of ten by fellow Mexican Rodolfo Ortega. Canto left the sport with a record of seventy-four fights (winning sixty-one, losing nine, and drawing four). Canto also fought the full distance of fifteen rounds more often than any other fighter in world flyweight title bouts, be it as champion or challenger—the total number being seventeen times.

A massive upset took place on 4 September 1982 at the Cobo Hall in Detroit, Michigan. Former undisputed world lightweight champion and former WBC world welterweight king Roberto Duran of Panama stepped into the ring to meet former British welterweight champion, Kirkland Laing. Duran was looking to re-establish himself after losing a fifteen-round points decision to Puerto Rican Wilfred Benitez on 30 January 1982 when challenging for the WBC world super-welterweight crown. While Laing was a talented boxer, it had to be said that he had up to that moment in time not met a fighter of Duran's calibre, so the chances of a Laing victory looked slim. Indeed, the chances of him even lasting the full ten rounds looked even slimmer. When summing up the contest, it looked a reasonably easy outing for Duran. However, on the night, Laing showed that he was not a man to dismiss and pulled off a surprise when he outboxed Duran to win a points decision.

On 18 September 1982, Charlie Magri of the UK ventured to the Cattle Market in Aviles, Spain to put his European flyweight crown on the line against Enrique Rodriguez Cal. This was the second meeting for the pair. The Spanish fighter had previously challenged Magri for the title on 24 February 1981 at the Royal Albert Hall in London. The fight proved to be an easy assignment for Magri, who stopped his man in two rounds in a contest scheduled for twelve. This time around, it appeared the challenge from Cal would be more taxing since he had all the comforts of home, performing in front of his fans. The fans giving him strong vocal support could very well inspire him to rise to the occasion and last the full distance of twelve rounds. Amazingly, Cal was once again defeated in the second session by the hard-punching defending champion.

Another member of the Feeney family won a British title on 12 October 1982 when George joined his younger brother, John, winning the domestic lightweight crown from holder Ray Cattouse via a fourteen-round stoppage in a contest slated for fifteen. The venue for the bout was the Royal Albert Hall in London. John had previously joined the ranks of British champions at York Hall in Bethnal Green, London, when winning the vacant British bantamweight crown on 22 September 1981. Feeney had stopped Dave Smith in round eight of a contest scheduled for fifteen rounds to ascend to the throne.

Patrizio Oliva won the European superlightweight crown in front of his home fans on 5 January 1983 when he boxed his way to a twelve-round points decision over holder Robert Gambini of France at Ischia Campania in Italy. On 27 March 1985, Oliva made his final defence against fellow countryman Alessandro Scapecchi at Nocere in Campania, Italy, outpointing his challenger over twelve rounds before relinquishing the crown. Oliva had been an outstanding champion, creating at the time a record of making eight successful consecutive defences of the title.

On 15 March 1983, Charlie Magri revealed all his fighting spirit when he won the WBC version of the world flyweight title in an exciting battle. It was not an easy fight for Magri, who battled against a game and determined champion in the shape of Eleonicio Mercedes of the Dominican Republic. However, Magri prevailed when he stopped Mercedes in round seven. The contest, which took place at Wembley Arena, was something of a historical event since it was the first WBC world title fight in the weight division to be scheduled for the duration of twelve rounds rather than fifteen.

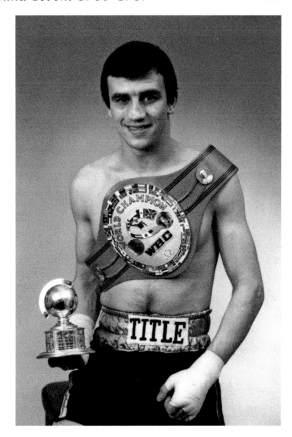

Charlie Magri won the WBC
world flyweight crown in
1983. (*Derek Rowe*)

Bobby Berna of the Philippines found his place in the sun when, on 4 December 1983, he became the first holder of the IBF world super-bantamweight title. The venue for the vacant championship fight took place in Seoul, South Korea. Berna put his name in the record books when opponent Sung-In Suh of South Korea was stopped in the tenth stanza of a contest scheduled for fifteen.

Dodie Boy Penalosa of the Philippines became the first world light-flyweight champion for the IBF on 10 December 1983. To do so, Penalosa had to enter his opponent's turf at the Osaka-Jo Hall in Osaka, Japan. Despite the local support for home fighter Satoshi Shingaki, Penalosa was able to gain victory with a twelve-round stoppage in a bout scheduled for fifteen.

Northern Ireland's Hugh Russell captured the British flyweight championship on 25 January 1984 when Welsh holder Kelvin Smart retired in round seven of twelve in a contest staged at the King's Hall in Belfast. Russell made history in this fast-paced encounter as he became the first fighter to win this title, having first held the British bantamweight crown.

On 28 March 1984, Scottish-born Murray Sutherland became the first holder of a world super-middleweight crown when he outpointed American Ernie Singletary over fifteen rounds for the IBF inaugural title. The contest took place at the Harrah's Marina Hotel Casino in Atlantic City, New Jersey. This was Sutherland's third attempt to win world honours. On 25 April 1981, he had a crack at the WBC light-heavyweight belt held by American Matthew Saad Muhammad at the Resorts International in Atlantic City, New Jersey. The challenge ended in round nine of fifteen when the champion retained his title by way of a knockout. At the Playboy Hotel and Casino in Atlantic City, New Jersey, on 11 April 1982, Sutherland had a shot at the WBA light-heavyweight version of the world title, only to come up a short once again when stopped in round eight of a scheduled fifteen by reigning champion Michael Spinks of America. Stepping down to a lower weight division proved to be a successful move for Sutherland.

The inaugural commonwealth title bout for the cruiserweight crown took place on 14 May 1984 between Britain's Stewart Lithgo and Australian Steve Aczel at the Festival Hall in Brisbane, Queensland. Aczel had the advantage of fighting on home turf and it could be said that he was favoured to win the title, but Lithgo sprang a surprise and won the championship by a stoppage victory in round eleven of twelve.

It looked like an easy night for Joe Frazier Jr on 27 October 1984 when he came to the Stormont Maine Club in Gateshead, Newcastle. Frazier Jr was paired with Briton Peter Eubank (brother of future WBO middleweight and super-middleweight world champion Chris Eubank). Frazier Jr (the son of former world heavyweight champion great Joe Frazier) was a competent performer with a record of twelve wins with just the one defeat. Eubank had paid a visit to the ring on twenty occasions (winning nine and losing eleven). Most expected Eubank to make his way home after the fight with another defeat on his record but in the bout, he produced an upset when he scored a ten-round points victory over his American opponent.

There have been times when the most anticipated fights have not lived up to expectations with pundits feeling somewhat disappointed. This could not be said of the bout between Marvin Hagler and Thomas Hearns, which took place at the Caesars Palace Outdoor Arena in Las Vegas, Nevada, on 15 April 1985. Hagler was defending his undisputed world middleweight crown against Hearns, a former WBA world welterweight king and reigning WBC super welter champion. Going into the ring, Hagler had an impressive professional record of sixty-four fights with sixty victories, two defeats, and two draws. Hearns entered the fray with a tally of forty-one bouts with one defeat. When the bell sounded to start the fight, Hagler came straight after his challenger who was quickly pinned on the ropes. There was an exchange of punches that saw the defending champion cut on the forehead; this was not a good start for Hagler. The action was breathtaking, with the two gladiators throwing punches like there was no tomorrow, both looking for a quick and decisive win. There was no way this battle was going to last the full duration of twelve rounds someone had to bend someone had to break and so it proved when Hagler found the punch in the third round to bring the fight to its conclusion. Hearns was put on the deck by a Hagler and upon rising to his feet was rightly considered by the referee to be in no fit state to carry on. The contest may have ended early but no one felt short-changed or complained; this particular championship bout provided more action in three rounds than many twelve or fifteen rounders had in the past. This was one championship fight that would be long remembered by the fans.

On 24 April 1985, Herol Graham won the vacant British middleweight title in devastating style when he knocked out opponent Jimmy Price in the opening session of a twelve-round contest. The venue for the contest was the Britannia Leisure Centre in Shoreditch, London. Graham therefore became the first British super-welterweight champion to move up a division to capture this crown. Graham was also a former European and Commonwealth super-welterweight title-holder.

At the Pier Pavillion in Hastings, Sussex, Prince Rodney climbed between the ropes to challenge Jimmy Cable for the British super-welterweight crown on 11 May 1985. The bout was set for twelve rounds, but Rodney quickly ended the fight, knocking out his opponent in the opening session. With this victory, Rodney became the first boxer to regain the domestic title in this division. Prince first won the championship, which was then vacant, on 11 October 1983 at the Royal Albert Hall in London when he fought former champion Jimmy Batten stopping him in round nine of twelve. Rodney later relinquished he crown.

On 8 June 1985, Panama's Eusebio Pedroza lost his WBA world featherweight crown to Ireland's Barry McGuigan in an exciting contest that took place at Loftus Road Stadium in Shepherd's Bush, London. The bout went the full fifteen rounds with both fighters giving their all and laying it on the line. A great deal was expected from McGuigan, who did not disappoint his many supporters on this very special night. Prior to this defeat, Pedroza had been a dominant champion who had made an impressive nineteen successive defences of the title after taking the crown from Spain's Cecilio Lastra by a thirteen-round stoppage in a scheduled fifteen at the Gimnasio Nuevo in Panama on 15 April 1978. The number of defences made by Pedroza was at the time a record for the division.

Above: Howard Winstone (left) with Marvin Hagler, who successfully defended his world middleweight crown against Thomas Hearns in 1985. (*Les Clark*)

Left: Herol Graham won the vacant British middleweight championship in 1985. (*Derek Rowe*)

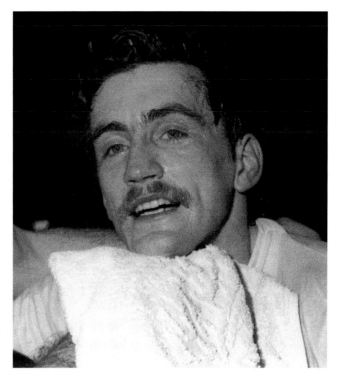

Barry McGuigan
defeated the
long-reigning
Eusebio Pedroza
to win the WBA
world featherweight
crown in 1985.
(*Derek Rowe*)

American Dwight Muhammad Qawi ventured to South Africa in his
bid to win the WBA world cruiserweight title. The battle took place at
the Sun City Superbowl in the North West Province, South Africa, on 27
July 1985. The defending champion Piet Crous was fighting in front of
his home fans and thus had all the support. Despite this, Qawi proved
to be the better man on the night and powered on to a most impressive
victory. Crous was outfought in a contest slated for fifteen rounds and
was knocked out in the eleventh session. Qawi achieved the distinction of
being the first former world light-heavyweight champion (WBC) to win a
major version of a world crown in this division.

A number of fighters who over the years had held or who were at
the time holding the world light-heavyweight crown had stepped up
into the bigger division and attempted to win the world heavyweight
championship. All their efforts had been futile with the established
heavyweight champion constantly proving to be too talented and too
strong. On 21 September 1985, Michael Spinks of America (the then
reigning WBC, WBA and IBF light-heavyweight title-holder) entered the
ring at the Riviera Hotel and Casino outdoor arena in Las Vegas, Nevada,
to challenge fellow countryman Larry Holmes, the reigning IBF king and
former WBC champion. This looked a tough ask for the challenger, with

the forecast being that Holmes would notch up another victory. However, this is boxing and history has shown that upsets often happen inside the ring. Spinks rose to the occasion on the night and added to the list of upsets, thus springing a surprise when he outpointed the defending heavyweight champion over fifteen rounds to become the first holder at light-heavyweight to accomplish this feat. Spinks showed that the big boys can be beaten. A return bout with Holmes took place on 19 April 1986 at the Hilton Center in Las Vegas, Nevada. Many felt that this time around, Holmes would get revenge and take back his crown; however, Spinks once got the better of the former champion and gained the victory with a fifteen-round decision.

Sammy Reeson became the first holder of the British cruiserweight crown on 31 October 1985 when he outpointed Stewart Lithgo, the former commonwealth king, over twelve rounds in a contest that took place at the Latchmere Leisure Centre in Wandsworth, London. In another inaugural championship bout, Reeson showed that he had not finished winning titles when he scored the double by becoming the first European title-holder at the weight when he defeated Germany's Manfred Jassmann at the Royal Albert Hall on 22 April 1987 by way of a twelve-round points decision.

On 17 April 1986, Pat Cowdell used his classy boxing skills to win the British super-featherweight title by stopping holder John Doherty in round six in a contest scheduled for twelve at the St George's Hall in Bradford, Yorkshire. On so doing, Cowdell became the first holder of the British featherweight crown to move up a weight division and capture this championship.

Dennis Andries became the first British fighter to twice regain a world title. Andries first won the WBC world light-heavyweight championship when he outpointed American J. B. Williamson over twelve rounds at Picketts Lock stadium in Edmonton, London, on 30 April 1986. Andries made a second defence of the title when he ventured to the USA on 7 March 1987. Andries was not going to have an easy ride as he was to meet the hard-hitting American challenger Thomas Hearns. Hearns was an outstanding fighter and was hence expected by many to win the crown. This Hearns did when he proved too much for the defending champion at the Cobo Hall in Detroit, Michigan. Andries gave it his all and went down fighting like a true champion, but the American won the title by a knockout in round ten of a scheduled twelve. This was not the end for Andries; on 21 February 1989, he contested the then-vacant WBC crown against American Tony Willis. While a good fighter, Willis was nowhere near the class of Hearns and subsequently looked to be a much easier task for Andries and a win for the former champion looked likely. The Briton regained the crown winning the title by a five-round stoppage of twelve at the Convention Center in Tucson, Arizona. Andries now looked like having a lengthy reign but his first defence on 24 June 1989 at the Convention Centre in Atlantic City, New Jersey, saw him lose the WBC title to Australian Jeff Harding, who stopped him in round twelve. Dennis then travelled down under to Australia and on 28 July 1990 at the Rod Laver Arena, Melbourne, Victoria, in a return with Jeff Harding, he regained the championship for the second time by way of a knockout in round seven in a bout set for twelve.

The fans at Wembley Arena in London witnessed a battle between the two top flyweights in the domestic division on 20 May 1986 in a double championship fight. The two protagonists were the reigning British champion Duke McKenzie and the ruling European and former British and WBC world title-holder Charlie Magri. The two gave the spectators a rousing encounter, which concluded when the Duke became a king when Magri retired in round five in a scheduled twelve. This was the first time that Magri had been beaten by a British opponent in the paid ranks and the last time he threw a punch inside the square ring. Magri later retired from the sport with an honourable record of thirty-five fights (winning thirty and losing five).

During his career, former world heavyweight champion Mike Tyson of America participated in fifty-eight professional bouts of which he

Dennis Andries in action (left) won the WBC world light-heavyweight championship three times during his career. (*Les Clark*)

won fifty and lost six, with two resulting in a no contest decision. Tyson finished twenty-three of his bouts inside the opening round (this included a disqualification victory). The fastest win of all for the former world title-holder came on 26 July 1986 at the Civic Center at Glen Falls, New York, when the man to fall to the heavy-punching Tyson was Marvis Frazier, who was halted in thirty seconds of the opening round in a contest optimistically scheduled for the duration of ten rounds.

It looked like an impossible mission when British fighter Lloyd Honeyghan went to the USA on 27 September 1986 to challenge Donald Curry for the undisputed world welterweight title. The venue for the contest was Caesars Hotel and Casino in Atlantic City, New Jersey. Both fighters were undefeated. Honeyghan had a tally of twenty-seven bouts without a blemish and along the way had won the British, European, and Commonwealth crowns. Curry also had a perfect record of twenty-five bouts without a loss. The American champion looked unbeatable—an elite boxer who had met a range of much higher calibre opponents than had his challenger. Curry's name looked like it was going to be added to the greats in the division. One of the fighters would lose their undefeated record in the meeting and it was felt that it would not be the American. It appeared that Honeyghan would be swept aside by Curry and would be lucky to hear the final bell. On the night, the British challenger did not take heed of the doom and gloom predictions; he was full of confidence, swagger, and self-belief entering the ring. Honeyghan's confidence was well founded since he not only shocked the defending champion but the boxing world when he stormed to a magnificent win, putting in an incredulous performance to stop Curry in the sixth round of twelve to give British boxing one of its best victories at that time.

Norway's Magne Havnaa made his professional debut on 3 October 1986 at the Idraetshuset in Copenhagen, Denmark. Havnaa's opponent was England's Johnny Nelson, who had fought twice prior to this meeting, losing both bouts on points. Nelson was to lose once again when Havnaa won a four-round points decision. The two fighters would go on from this contest and have successful careers, both winning the WBO version of the world cruiserweight championship.

A hurricane blew in and hit Las Vegas on 22 November 1986. There was no advanced weather broadcast about this destructive force. No one could blame the meteorologists since this particular hurricane was of the human variety in the shape an American called Mike Tyson, who punched his way in whirlwind fashion to the WBC heavyweight championship of the world by stopping defending champion Trevor Berbick of Canada. Berbick felt the full brunt of this particular storm and was blown away when stopped in two rounds of a contest set for twelve at the Hilton Hotel. Berbick had no answer to the hard-punching challenger who in relentless fashion

Lloyd Honeyghan (left) is seen looking for an opening to land his punches against his opponent; he won the undisputed world welterweight title in 1986. (*Les Clark*)

walked through him with comparative ease. Tyson came into the ring with a record of twenty-seven victories, with twenty-five inside the distance to challenge the title-holder. The victory gave Tyson the distinction of becoming (at the age of twenty-one years, four months, and twenty-three days) the youngest man to win a version of the heavyweight title.

Jimmy Ellis Jr boxed for the last time in the professional ring on 9 February 1987 when, in a ten-round contest, he was stopped by opponent and fellow American Joe McKnight in round three. The bout was staged at the Landmark Hotel in Metairie, Louisiana. Ellis Jr had comprised a record of eight bouts (winning six and losing two). Ellis Jr failed to reach the heights of his father who was the former WBA world heavyweight king Jimmy Ellis.

At the Festival Hall, Super Tent, Basildon on 4 March 1987, Terry Marsh picked his punches well and won the IBF world super-lightweight crown when he defeated American title-holder Joe Manley, who he stopped in round ten of fifteen. In so doing, Marsh became the first British boxer to hold a world championship in this weight division since Jack Kid Berg, who reigned from 1930–31.

He was an outstanding fighter—a modern-day great who oozed class when in action. This fact was confirmed by his boxing record, which revealed thirty-four fights with just one defeat. A former undisputed world welterweight and WBA super-welterweight champion, his name was Sugar Ray Leonard. Despite his overwhelming ring talents, he was considered an underdog when he faced the reigning world middleweight title-holder on 6 April 1987. Marvin Hagler was the boss of the division; he was the man and, like Leonard, was considered a great. Hagler looked unbeatable in the division. Those who had previously attempted to take his crown were painfully shown the errors of their way. When two greats meet like this, the interest in the fight captures the imagination of the public and the sport receives a great deal of media coverage. Hagler was defending his crown for the thirteenth time with a slate of sixty-six bouts with two defeats and two draws; he was fully expected to leave the ring at the Caesars Palace Outdoor Arena in Las Vegas, Nevada, with his crown firmly on his head. Once again, as it often does in boxing, a surprise took place when Leonard took the championship, being awarded a twelve-round points decision. Prior to the contest, Hagler had relinquished the WBA and IBF versions of the title. Leonard only won the WBC belt when defeating Hagler, but followers of the sport knew that with this victory, Leonard had become the genuine world champion with or without the WBA and IBF belts.

On 4 June 1987, John Feeney threw his last punch in the professional ring, outpointing opponent Nigel Senior over eight rounds. The contest took place at the Crowtree Leisure Centre in Sunderland, Tyne and Wear. Feeney had an honourable career and left the sport with a record of forty-eight bouts (winning thirty-five and losing thirteen). During his time punching for pay, Feeney captured the British bantamweight crown twice. However, the European title eluded Feeney; try as he may, he failed to add the championship to his name. Feeney attempted to take the title four times and each of the respective challenges took place on away turf in Italy. The first time took place on 17 June 1981 at Cervia, Emilia-Romagna against holder Valerio Nati, who held on to his crown via a twelve-round points decision. Challenge number two came on 30 June 1982 against the reigning king Giuseppe Fossati at the Campobello di Mazara in Sicily; once again, Feeney came back to the UK empty-handed when the Italian champion earned a twelve-round points verdict. At the Campobasso, Molise on 28 December 1983, Feeney climbed between the ropes in his bid to become king of Europe when he battled Valter Giorgetti and once again, the decision went against him in a bout that went the full twelve rounds. The fourth and final attempt saw Feeney cross gloves for the then-vacant title against Ciro De Leva on 14 November 1984 at Salerno, Camania; yet again, the decision on points favoured the home fighter after twelve rounds. Had Feeney been given home ground advantage in one of his challenges, it is possible he might well have won the championship in one of his bids.

The first contest for a world title in the minimumweight division took place on 14 June 1987 between South Korea's Kyung-Yung Lee and Japan's Masaharu Kawakami, who contested the IBF version of the championship. Lee, who was engaging in his eleventh professional contest, did so with an undefeated record, while Kawakami was taking part in his first bout in the paid ranks. Unsurprisingly, due to his opponent's lack of experience, Lee emerged victorious when he knocked out Kawakami in the second round of fifteen to claim the title.

American challenger and former WBA world super-lightweight champion Gene Hatcher arrived in Spain to battle Britain's Lloyd Honeyghan for the world welterweight crown on 30 August 1987. Honeyghan was making the third defence of the WBC and IBF titles and looked the firm favourite to retain them. However, the American looked capable of giving the champion a good argument while the bout lasted. At the Plaza de Toros de Nueva, Andalucia, the fans settled in to watch the contest but must have been just a little shocked on just how quickly the twelve-round contest ended since it was all over in a reported forty-five seconds of the opening round. This created a record at the time for being the fastest win in a world welterweight title fight.

Jeff Fenech became the first Australian to win a world championship in three weight divisions on 7 March 1988. At the Entertainment Centre in Sydney, he met opponent Victor Callejas of Puerto Rico for the vacant WBC world featherweight title and emerged victorious when the referee stopped the contest in round ten of a scheduled twelve. Fenech was a former holder of the IBF world bantamweight and WBC world super-bantamweight titles.

The super-middleweight division saw its first southpaw world champion crowned on 11 March 1988 when Graciano Rocchigiani battled his way to the vacant IBF crown in front of his home fans at the Philips Halle in Düsseldorf, Germany. Vincent Boulware of America was the opponent who was stopped in the eighth session of a contest set for fifteen.

On 9 April 1988, American Evander Holyfield (the WBA and IBF world cruiserweight champion) met Carlos De Leon of Puerto Rico (the reigning WBC title-holder) in a unification contest at Caesars Pavilion in Las Vegas. Holyfield confirmed that he was without doubt the number one fighter in this poundage when he punched his way to victory, stopping his opponent in round eight of twelve. In doing so, Holyfield achieved the feat of becoming the first fighter in the division to become the undisputed world champion.

On 9 May 1988, Khaokor Galaxy of Thailand won the WBA world bantamweight crown via a twelve-round points decision against the defending champion, Wilfredo Vazquez of Puerto Rico. The contest took place at the Hua Mark Indoor Stadium in Bangkok, Thailand. The victory by Galaxy secured its place in boxing history as for the first time, two twin brothers held a world championship simultaneously. Khaokor's sibling, Khaosai Galaxy, was the reigning WBA world super-flyweight title-holder.

On 27 June 1988, the scene was set for Mike Tyson to defend his world heavyweight title against Michael Spinks, the former undisputed world light-heavyweight and IBF heavyweight king at the Convention Hall in Atlantic City, New Jersey. Both men were undefeated: Tyson in thirty-four bouts, Spinks in thirty-one. It was expected that Spinks would give Tyson a hard battle. However, Tyson had an easy night, winning by a knockout in the opening round in a contest set for twelve. The fight was all over in one minute and thirty-one seconds.

Marvis Frazier had his last ring battle on 27 October 1988 at the Convention Center in Tucson, Arizona, outpointing fellow American Philipp Brown over ten rounds. Marvis (the son of the great former world heavyweight champion Joe Frazier) left the boxing scene with a respectable record consisting of nineteen wins with two defeats. The two setbacks in his career came when he was stopped twice in the first round. The first crushing defeat came on 25 November 1983 when he stepped into the ring with reigning WBC world heavyweight king Larry Holmes at Caesars Palace Sports Pavilion, Las Vegas. Since Frazier was not ranked in the WBC world rankings, the organisation did not sanction the fight, so it was a twelve-round, non-title dust-up. Had Frazier won, the WBC would have stripped Holmes of the crown and declared the championship vacant. There was no fear of that happening since it was all over in the opening session as Holmes was far superior. The next prompt exit came on 26 July 1986 at the Civic Center Glenn Falls in New York, the opponent being future undisputed world heavyweight king Mike Tyson. The bout was set for the duration of ten rounds. However, Tyson ruthlessly dispatched Frazier in the opening stanza without working up a sweat. It was really obvious now that Marvis would not emulate his father and win a world heavyweight title during his career.

At the Las Vegas Hilton on 4 November 1988, Thomas Hearns became the first holder of the WBO version of the world super-middleweight crown when he outpointed fellow American James Kinchen over twelve rounds to capture the vacant crown. At that time, Hearns was no stranger to winning world championship belts as he was a former world champion in the following divisions: WBA welterweight, WBC super-welterweight, WBC light-heavyweight, and WBC middleweight.

A rarity in world championship bouts took place on 7 November 1988, when two belts from different weight divisions were contested at the same time. American Sugar Ray Leonard confronted Donny Lalonde for the

WBC world light-heavyweight crown, which the Canadian was defending, and the inaugural WBC world super-middleweight title, which was also at stake. The contest, which took place at Caesars Palace, Las Vegas, saw Leonard stop his opponent in round nine of twelve to add to his collection of championship belts. At that moment in time, the American had previously held the WBC and WBA world welterweight titles, the WBA super-welterweight crown, and the WBC world middleweight championship. Sugar Ray was already considered to be one of the greats in boxing.

American Michael Moorer became the first holder of the WBO version of the world light-heavyweight crown when he impressively put his punches together and hence found the finishing blow to stop Jordan-born Ramzi Hassan in round five of twelve. The contest took place at the Brook Park in Ohio on 3 December 1988.

In a bout for the first WBO version of the world middle title Americans Doug DeWitt and Robbie Sims laced up the gloves to face each other at the Showboat Hotel and Casino in Atlantic City, New Jersey, on 18 April 1989. At the end of a good solid twelve-round contest, DeWitt took the decision on points to be the new king. At that moment, the rival world champions were Michael Nunn (IBF), WBA title was vacant, and Roberto Duran (WBC).

American Kenny Mitchell ascended to the WBO world super-bantamweight throne on 29 April 1989 at the Roberto Clemente Coliseum in San Juan, Puerto Rico, when he defeated local fighter Julio Gervacio by a twelve-round points decision. By defeating Gervacio, Mitchell became the first WBO world champion in this weight division.

Jose de Jesús of Puerto Rico became the first holder of the WBO version of the world light-flyweight crown on 19 May 1989 when he contested the inaugural crown with opponent Fernando Martinez of Mexico. The contest took place at the El San Juan Hotel and Casino in San Juan, Puerto Rico. De Jesús became the champion when he was given a nine-round technical points decision in a bout set for twelve.

On 3 June 1989, Glenn McCrory created a very special day for himself when he became the first British fighter to hold a version of the world cruiserweight title. McCrory put in an outstanding performance to capture the vacant IBF crown at the Louisa Centre in Stanley, County Durham by outpointing Kenya Patrick Lumumba over twelve exciting rounds. A successful defence of the championship followed on 21 October 1989, when the Briton found the punch to end the contest, knocking out challenger Siza Makathini of South Africa in round eleven of twelve at the Eston Sports Academy in Middlesborough. McCrory looked to have all the ingredients to have a long reign as champion but in boxing, situations can change so very quickly. McCrory's reign came to a sharp and abrupt end on 22 March 1990 at the Gateshead Leisure Centre in Tyne and Wear when American Jeff Lampkin landed his damaging punches to ensure the crown was going to return with him to the USA. McCrory was knocked out in round three in a contest set for twelve rounds. After this bout, McCrory boxed on, winning three, losing one, and drawing one of his next five contests. However, Glenn had another chance at the championship when he travelled to Russia in an attempt to regain the IBF crown on 16 July 1993 but failed in his task when outpointed over twelve rounds by the then reigning champion American Alfred Cole at the CSKA in Moscow.

Clinton McKenzie called time on his professional career on 12 August 1989 when he failed to regain the European super-lightweight title from Italian holder Efrem Calamati; the venue was Sansepolcro in Toscana, Italy. McKenzie had comprised a record of fifty bouts (winning thirty-six and losing fourteen); he had created two records before he bid farewell to the sport. The first record was that he was the first boxer in the division to win the British super-lightweight crown on three separate occasions. McKenzie first won the British title when he paid a visit to Maysfield Leisure Centre in Belfast, Northern Ireland, to contest the vacant title with local fighter Jim Montague on 11 October 1978, winning the championship by a knockout in round ten of a contest scheduled for fifteen. Challenger Colin Powers deprived McKenzie of the domestic title when he outpointed him over fifteen rounds on 6 February 1979 at the Conference Centre, London. It was revenge time for McKenzie on 11 September 1979 when once again at the Conference Centre, the two crossed gloves for the second time, with McKenzie, this time coming out on top with a fifteen-round points decision to once again become champion of Britain. In his fifth defence of his second reign, on 19 September 1984, he shared the ring with Terry Marsh at the Britannia Leisure Centre in Shoreditch, London, and found himself a former title-holder for the second time when losing the crown by way of a twelve-round points decision. McKenzie had two failed attempts to regain the title after the Marsh defeat. This however was not the end for McKenzie championship wise as on 24 January 1989, he stepped up once again to challenge for the title. For the third time, he took the domestic throne when he outpointed holder Lloyd Christie over twelve rounds at the King's Heath Leisure Centre in Birmingham. McKenzie's second record of note was his participating in more British super-lightweight championship bouts at that time than any other fighter, the total being eleven in all.

On 19 September 1989, Northern Ireland's Sam Storey became the first domestic champion at the super-middleweight poundage. Storey (who entered the fray with a record of thirteen bouts: winning twelve and losing one) achieved this feat by outpointing London's Tony Burke over twelve rounds. Burke had a slate that comprised twenty-five fights (winning fourteen and losing eleven). The entertaining contest took place at the Ulster Hall in Belfast, Northern Ireland.

American Michael Moorer dispatched his challenger Mexican-born Mike Sedillo in the sixth session of a twelve-round contest in defence of his WBO world light-heavyweight crown on 22 December 1989. The contest took place at The Palace in Auburn Hills, Michigan. Moorer was a busy champion and his defeat of Sedillo gave him the distinction of making the most defences of the light-heavyweight championship in any one calendar year at that time. The total number of defences made by Moorer in 1989 was six.

8

Round Eight:
1990–1999

American Anthony Witherspoon had a bad night at the Gateshead Leisure Centre in Gateshead, Tyne and Wear on 22 March 1990. His scheduled eight-round bout with Briton Dave Garside ended when he retired from the contest in round six. It was apparent that Anthony's boxing career was not going to reach the dizzy heights of brother Tim Witherspoon who twice won a version of the world heavyweight title: first the WBC and then the WBA. Witherspoon left the sport with a professional record of nineteen victories with seven defeats.

The UK proved to be a successful hunting ground for Jamaican-born Mike McCallum who won two world title bouts in said country. McCallum also a former WBA world super-welterweight champion defended his WBA world middleweight crown at the Royal Albert Hall, Kensington, on 14 April 1990 against two of the leading British fighters at the time. Reigning Commonwealth title-holder Michael Watson was a worthy challenger for the championship and looked to be in with a chance of taking the title. McCallum was very highly regarded and proved that his reputation was well-deserved when he put his punches together to retain his title against his British challenger. Watson gave his all but tasted defeat when knocked out in round eleven of twelve in an absorbing contest. McCallum had previously won the vacant WBA title on 10 May 1989 also at the Royal Albert Hall when outpointing the then British middleweight and former European middleweight and British, European, and Commonwealth super-welterweight king Herol Graham over twelve rounds.

During his illustrious boxing career, Britain's Nigel Benn won versions of a world title in two different weight divisions, on both occasions doing so the hard way in the defending champion's own country—no easy feat

Mike McCallum won two world
middleweight championship
fights in the UK during his career.
(*Les Clark*)

at the best of times. Nigel won his first world crown in the USA on 29 April 1990 at the Caesars Hotel and Casino in Atlantic City, New Jersey, in an exciting duel in which he eventually stopped American holder Doug DeWitt in round eight of twelve to capture the WBO middleweight title. The second championship came when Benn stepped up a division and stopped Italian Mauro Galvano (the defending title-holder) in three rounds in a contest set for twelve on 3 October 1992 to win the WBC version of the world super-middleweight crown at the Palaghiaccio de Marino in Lazio, Italy.

Massimiliano Duran brought the WBC world cruiserweight crown to Italy when he defeated the defending champion Carlos De Leon of Puerto Rico on 27 July 1990 by a disqualification in round eleven. De Leon's offence was he hit his challenger after the bell had sounded to end the session in a contest set for twelve. The battle between the two took place at the Outdoor Arena in Capo d'Orlando, Sicily. Duran was the son of former European super-welterweight and two-time European middleweight king Juan Carlos Duran and the older brother of Alessandro who also found success in the ring. The younger sibling during his career won the European welterweight championship and in the same division the lightly regarded WBU crown.

Nigel Benn won
both his world
title bouts abroad:
WBO middleweight
(1980) and WBC
super-middleweight
(1992). (*Les Clark*)

The battle for the vacant WBC world middleweight title, which took place on 24 November 1990, between Julian Jackson from the Virgin Islands and Britain's Herol Graham was filled with drama. The fight finished with a remarkable come-from-behind knockout, which made the judges' points inconsequential. A former holder of the WBA super-welterweight crown, Jackson entered the ring at the Torrequebrada Hotel and Casino in Andalucia, Spain with a record of forty-one fights with one defeat. Graham too had an excellent tally of forty-three bouts and two defeats. To date, Herol had won the British, European, and Commonwealth super-welterweight and British and European middleweight titles and with his ability looked fated to win even further honours in the sport. Once the bell sounded to start the fight, Graham proved his boxing superiority, winning the first two rounds with ease, banging in some damaging blows to hurt his opponent. At the end of the third round, the ringside doctor took a long and hard look at Jackson; it appeared that Graham had the fight all but won and he was on the glorious path to being crowned world champion. Jackson was ready for the taking—of that, there was no mistake. However, one punch can change the course of a fight in an instant and this was one such occurrence. When the fourth round of twelve commenced, Jackson was allowed to continue; Graham came out for the finish and attacked ferociously, pinning his man on the ropes. The end looked near, and it was—but for Graham instead of Jackson. The contest concluded in an unexpected manner, which would have suited a Hollywood boxing film, but even then, many of the audience viewing the movie might have found it a little too far-fetched to believe. However, there is an old saying that truth is often stranger than fiction, and this was one such example. Jackson threw a punch that landed clean on Graham's jaw, which chillingly knocked him out cold; the Briton was unconscious before he hit the canvas. Be it a lucky punch thrown in desperation or a calculated and well-timed blow, it made very little difference; Jackson was the victor and new title-holder in an amazing contest.

On 5 March 1991, Gary De'Roux won the British featherweight championship in an action-packed contest. De'Roux was a fearless performer who came forward throughout the contest and attacked defending title-holder Sean Murphy relentlessly. The challenger would not be denied and round after round continuously drove the title-holder back

Herol Graham came close to winning the vacant WBC world middleweight title in 1990.
(*Derek Rowe*)

with hurtful punches to both head and body. It appeared very obvious that the championship bout would not run the full course of twelve rounds. This conclusion was confirmed when the fight ended with De'Roux knocking out the title-holder in round five. The contest was staged at the London Arena in Millwall. On the night, De'Roux became the first boxer from Peterborough to win a British title. The new champion was born in Manchester but was a resident of Peterborough.

Wally Swift Jr showed that the apple does not fall too far from the tree when it comes to boxing. Swift Jr showed his pugilistic ability when he stopped opponent Ensley Bingham in round four of a scheduled twelve on 19 March 1991 to win the vacant British super-welterweight title. Swift Jr took the championship at the Central Hall in Birmingham. In so doing, Swift Jr kept the family tradition going since his father Wally Swift Sr had during his respective career in the professional ring captured a British crown in two different weight divisions (welterweight and middleweight).

On 29 October 1991, Colin McMillan retained his British featherweight title by outpointing former champion at the weight Sean Murphy over twelve rounds at the Royal Albert Hall, Kensington. In so doing, McMillan created a record at the time by winning the Lonsdale Belt outright faster than any other previous domestic title-holder in the division. The feat took five months and seven days. McMillan first won the crown on 22 May 1991 when he stopped defending king Gary De'Roux in round seven of a contest set for twelve at the London Arena, Millwall. The first defence took place on 4 September 1991 against former British super-featherweight title-holder Kevin Pritchard did not go the scheduled twelve rounds when McMillan retained his crown in round seven at the York Hall in Bethnal Green, London.

On 21 December 1991, Khaosai Galaxy of Thailand successfully defended his WBA world super-flyweight title at the Taepsapin Stadium in Bangkok, Thailand, outpointing Mexican challenger Armando Castro over twelve rounds. This proved to be Galaxy's last professional contest he departed from the sport with a record of forty-eight fights (winning forty-seven and losing one). Galaxy also defended the championship on nineteen concessive occasions—a record for the division at that time.

John Doherty lost the British super-featherweight title to Michael Armstrong by way of a stoppage in round seven of twelve on 25 April 1992 in a contest that took place at the G-Mex Centre in Manchester, Lancashire. This proved to be Doherty's last professional contest after participating in thirty-nine bouts (winning twenty-eight, losing eight, and drawing three). However, he left the ring with the distinction of being the first boxer at the time to win the super-featherweight title on three separate occasions. Doherty first won the championship on 16 January 1986 when he outpointed Pat Doherty (no relation) over twelve rounds at the Guild Hall in Preston, Lancashire. Doherty then lost the championship to Pat Cowdell on 17 April 1986 at the St Georges Hall in Bradford, Yorkshire, when stopped in six rounds in a contest set for twelve. The opportunity for Doherty to wear the crown once again took place on 6 September 1989 at the Afan Lido in Port Talbot, Wales, where the then-defending champion Floyd Havard retired in round eleven of twelve. Joey Jacobs then took the championship from Doherty with a twelve-round points decision on 6 February 1990 at the Sports Centre in Lord Street, Oldham, Lancashire. Many felt at the time that the championship days of Doherty were over. However, he was not a man to write off since on 19 September 1991, he outpointed the then-current holder Sugar Gibiliru over twelve rounds at the Town Hall in Stockport, Cheshire, to regain the crown.

Colin McMillan became the first British fighter to capture the WBO version of the world featherweight crown on 16 May 1992. McMillan (the British and Commonwealth champion) took on the highly talented Italian Maurizio Stecca, who was making the third defence of the title in his second reign as champion. Stecca came armed with a record of forty-four wins with just one defeat and had a good amateur career, which involved winning the Olympic gold medal at bantamweight at the 1984 Games, which were held in Los Angeles. While no mug himself in the ring, McMillan could not match the credentials of his opponent with a slate of twenty-two wins and one defeat. However, at the Alexandra Pavilion in Muswell Hill, London, McMillan confirmed that he belonged with the elite fighters in the division by outboxing the champion over twelve rounds to take the title.

Chris Eubank made a third successful defence of his WBO world super-middleweight title on 27 June 1992. The Briton outpointed American challenger Ron Essett over twelve rounds to retain his crown. Eubank boxed well within himself during the bout. The contest took place at the Hotel Quinto Do Lago. This event marked the first-ever world boxing championship to take place in Portugal.

The boxing MC was considered to be a role undertaken by man. A woman carrying out this duty was unheard of and hardly considered. However, Lisa Budd broke down this barrier when she became the first woman from the UK to become a boxing master of ceremonies. Lisa made her debut in this capacity on 17 September 1992 at Watford Town Hall in Hertfordshire.

On 15 October 1992, Duke McKenzie captured the WBO version of the world super-bantamweight title from American holder Jesse Benavides, outpointing him over the duration of twelve rounds at the Lewisham Theatre in London. In so doing, McKenzie became the first British-born fighter to win a world crown in three different weight divisions since Bob Fitzsimmons. Duke had previously held the IBF world flyweight title, capturing the crown on 5 October 1988 at the Gran Hall in Wembley, London. McKenzie knocked out the defending champion, Rolando Bohol of the Philippines, in round eleven of a slated twelve to ascend to the championship. Duke then took the WBO world bantamweight title, outpointing the champion, Gaby Canizales of America, over twelve rounds at the Elephant and Castle Centre in Southwark, London, on 30 June 1991.

On 16 October 1992, Gary Jacobs travelled across the channel to contest the vacant European welterweight title against opponent Ludovic Proto at the Salle Pierre de Coubertin in Paris, France. After twelve rounds of boxing, Proto was given the points decision. It looked as if the visiting Scot was given a raw deal with regards to the verdict. An immediate return took place on 6 February 1993. It was hoped that Jacobs would get his second chance at home in the UK but once again, Jacobs had to venture onto his opponent's turf in France. At the Cirque d'Hiver in Paris, the British fighter gained sweet revenge when he stopped his opponent in nine rounds of a scheduled twelve to capture the title. The win by Jacobs may not have produced a wave of fear among the elite fighters at the weight but then truthfully, no one expected it to. However, the victory did see Jacobs acquire a victory of significance since he became the first Scottish fighter to win the European welterweight title since Tommy Milligan, who reigned from 1924–1925.

At long last, Britain had a world heavyweight champion. It may be true to say that the coronation for the new king did not come the way many had expected it to, that being inside the ring. The then undisputed champion Riddick Bowe of America relinquished the WBC version of the title (he still held the WBA and IBF crowns) on 14 December 1992. The WBC then awarded the title to Lewis. This situation came about when an agreement for Bowe to fight Lewis failed to materialise. Lewis then became the first British-born holder of a world heavyweight title since Bob Fitzsimmons, who reigned from 1897 to 1899.

When Ruben Palacious of Columbia (who was due to defend his WBO World featherweight crown against England's John Davison) failed his medical, he had to relinquish his title. Welshman Steve Robinson was drafted in at short notice to fill the opposite corner of the ring against Davison in a contest for the vacant crown. Under the circumstances, Robinson appeared to have very little chance of winning the championship against the favoured Davison. It hence looked that at the end of the proposed contest, Davison would emerge the victor, be it on points or a stoppage. However, every now and then, boxing provides a fairy tale end, where the underdog proves to be the top dog and upsets the odds;

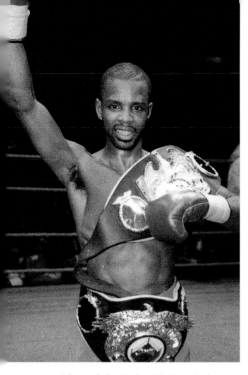

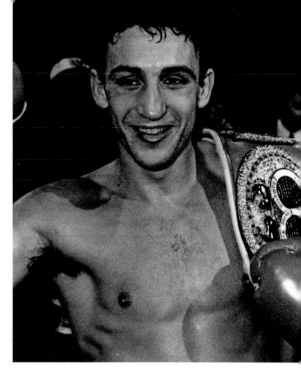

Above left: Duke McKenzie became the second British-born boxer to win a world title in three different weight divisions. (*Les Clark*)

Above right: Gary Jacobs won the European welterweight crown in 1993. (*Les Clark*)

Below: Walter McGowan (left) with Gary Jacobs and Bobby Neill. (*Derek Rowe*)

this was one such occasion. Robinson had learnt his trade the hard way, fighting a variety of opponents during his career, and was a consummate professional. The Welshman's skills inside the ring were often underrated, but in his meeting with Davison, he showed just how good he really was. The Welshman hence surprised everyone on the night of 17 April 1993 at the Northumbria Leisure Centre in Washington, Tyne and Wear. Making the most of his unexpected opportunity, Robinson claimed the title with a twelve-round points victory over his opponent. Robinson became the first Welsh boxer to hold a version this title since WBC king Howard Winstone, who both won and lost the title in 1968.

It is often said that size does not matter—a fact that Scotland's Paul Weir had good reason to celebrate when he became Britain's first holder of the world minimumweight title. The poundage was the smallest weight category in professional boxing. The contest took place at the Scottish Exhibition Centre in Glasgow on 15 May 1993. Weir boxed well and gave his fans plenty to cheer about when he stopped Mexico's Fernando Martinez in round seven of twelve to win the vacant WBO crown.

South Africa's Jacob Matlala won the WBO world flyweight crown on 15 May 1993 at the Scottish Exhibition Centre in Glasgow when he

Steve Robinson became an unexpected world champion in 1993. (*Les Clark*)

stopped defending champion Pat Clinton of Scotland in round eight of a scheduled twelve. Matlala won a second world title on 18 November 1995 when he dropped down a division to light-flyweight and challenged yet another Scot in the shape of Paul Weir, who surrendered his WBO title when he lost by a technical five-round decision of a bout set for the duration of twelve at the Kelvin Hall in Glasgow, Scotland. At the time, Matlata held the record of being the shortest man (at the listed height of 4 feet 10 ½ inches) to have won a world professional championship.

The ladies added another historic note to the pages of boxing history on 22 May 1993 when, for the first time three, female judges officiated at a world heavyweight title bout at the RFK Stadium in Washington D.C.: Shelia Harmon, Patricia Morse Jarman, and Jean Williams took their seats at ringside to score the WBA title defence of Riddick Bowe against challenger and fellow American Jessie Ferguson. However, they were saved the task of rendering a score when Bowe stopped his man in ultimate ease in two rounds of twelve. Bowe also held the IBF version of the championship, but this organisation refused to sanction the bout for their title.

On 6 August 1993, Gerald McClellan confidently stepped into the ring to defend his WBC world middleweight title against fellow American Jay Bell at the Coliseo Rubén Rodríguez in Bayamón, Puerto Rico. The confidence was not out of place since the heavy-handed McClellan knocked out his challenger in a reported twenty seconds of the first round of twelve, securing the fastest ever victory at the time in the division.

On 1 October 1993, Lennox Lewis defended his WBC world heavyweight crown against challenger Frank Bruno at the Cardiff Arms Park in Wales. The contest, when announced, caught fire with the public, who keenly welcomed the meeting between these two fighters. This contest was one for the history books as it was a historical event, being the first time that two British boxers had fought each other in a world heavyweight championship contest. It was also the first world heavyweight title fight to be staged in Wales. The title bout did not disappoint the many fans who turned up to see the event. It was action-packed from the first bell, with both men landing their share of heavy punches. Bruno looked dangerous in the early stages of the bout, giving the champion plenty to contend with; there were moments when it looked as if he was going to get the better of Lewis. However, the defending title-holder gradually got his act together and ended proceedings to impressively retain his crown when he stopped Bruno in round seven of twelve in a contest few expected to go the full distance one way or the other. The bout proved to be a hard-fought battle that spoke volumes for both fighters.

The vacant WBA world cruiserweight championship was up for grabs at the Cirque d'Hiver in Paris on 6 November 1993. The two fighters who stepped up to battle for the crown were American Orlin Norris and Marcelo

Victor Figueroa from Argentina. The two men battled until the sixth round in a bout set for twelve, when the vacancy for the title was filled as the contest was stopped. The man who had his gloved hand raised in victory was Norris, who thus joined his brother as a world title-holder. The younger sibling, Terry Norris, reigned at that time as the WBC super-welterweight champion.

It was all going so well for Mexico's Julio Cesar Chavez—an outstanding fighter who was clearly punching his way towards being one of the greats in the world of boxing. Stepping into the ring to defend his WBC world super-lightweight crown, the former holder of the WBC super-featherweight and WBA and WBC lightweight crowns looked as if he would extend his incredible undefeated record of eighty-nine wins and one draw ever further. That was not to underestimate his American challenger; Frankie Randall was a good ring exponent with a tally of forty-eight victories with two defeats and one draw. Against any other champion, you might have felt that Frankie was in with more than a mere shout, but this was not any other champion: it was Chavez, the man who was used to winning; defeat was not a word you would associate with his name. Chavez had that confident air about him; he was a master at his trade and was always fully in control in the ring. At the MGM Grand in Las Vegas on 29 January 1994, the spectators expected the obvious: a win for the Mexican. However, things did not go quite to plan. Randall proved to be more of a handful than first thought and this was his night; he provided a shock in outpointing the title-holder over twelve rounds to take the crown. Adding insult to injury, the challenger even became the first man in the paid ranks to floor Chavez for a count, putting him on the deck in round eleven.

During his career, Henry Wharton did extremely well, winning the British, European, and Commonwealth super-middleweight titles, but missed out on the world crown. No one can say that Wharton did not try; he had three attempts at the global championship against fellow Britons for the respective titles. Wharton's first challenge took place on 26 February 1994 against Nigel Benn for the WBC world super-middleweight belt at the Earls Court Exhibition Hall in Kensington, London, putting in a worthy effort but losing a twelve-round points decision. In the same year, on 10 December, Henry made a second bid, this time for Chris Eubank's WBO version of the title. The bout took place at the G-Mex Centre in Manchester; once again, Wharton went down to a twelve-round points decision. The third and final attempt to win a world championship took place on 3 May 1997 at the Nynex Arena in Manchester against defending WBC king Robin Reid. It was not a case of third time lucky since Wharton once again failed in his bid when outpointed over twelve rounds.

The fans at York Hall in Bethnal Green, London, on 5 April 1994 witnessed a contest that would not be called exciting it has to be said.

Henry Wharton, seen with his Commonwealth and European super-middleweight championship belts, failed to win a world crown. (*Les Clark*)

However, they did see in action two future world title-holders when reigning European heavyweight champion Henry Akinwande took part in a non-title contest, outpointing fellow Briton Johnny Nelson over ten rounds. Akinwande went on to successfully contest the vacant WBO world heavyweight crown on 29 June 1996 at the Fantasy Springs Casino in Indigo, California, when he knocked out American opponent Jeremy Williams in round three of a scheduled twelve. On 27 March 1999, Nelson challenged the reigning WBO world cruiserweight king Carl Thompson in an all-British clash at the Derby Storm Arena, winning by a five-round stoppage in a contest set for twelve.

Richie Wenton and Bradley Stone crossed swords on 26 April 1994 for the first-ever contest for the British super-bantamweight crown at York Hall. Wenton was crowned the king of the domestic division when he stopped Stone in round ten of a twelve round bout. However, sadly two days after the respective contest, Stone passed away due to a blood clot in the brain.

Italy's Vincenzo Belcastro lost his European bantamweight title to England's Naseem Hamed on 11 May 1994 at the Ponds Forge Arena in Sheffield by way of a twelve-round points decision. Like Hamed's previous opponents, Belcastro was not able to cope with his ultra-talented challenger who was always fully in control of the contest. Belcastro may have been a little disappointed in losing his crown but he had been a worthy champion during his title reign and was aware that he had lost to someone special. Belcastro was able to salvage something from the night for he left the ring after creating a record of having participated in more European title bouts in the division than any other boxer, the total being twelve in all. No doubt, he would have liked to have extended that record but it was not to be. Belcastro first won the crown on 13 April 1988 in fine style, knocking out French holder Fabrice Benichou in three rounds of twelve in Busalla, Italy. The Italian later lost the title in his sixth defence in Calais, France, to home fighter Thierry Jacob on points over twelve rounds. Belcastro then regained the vacant title on 27 January 1993, outpointing fellow countryman Antonio Picardi over twelve rounds in Orzinuovi, Italy. Then, once again, Belcastro lost his crown in his fourth defence to Hamed.

On 10 September 1994, Polish-born German fighter Dariusz Michalczewski won the WBO world light-heavyweight crown when he defeated Leeonzer Barber of America by way of a twelve round points decision at the Sporthalle, Alsterdoff in Hamburg, Germany. During the course of his professional career, Michalczewski also captured the WBA and IBF versions of the championship and also became a two-weight title-holder by winning the WBO world cruiserweight crown on 17 December 1994, knocking out defending champion Nestor Hipolito Giovannini of Argentina in round ten of twelve once again at the Sporthalle, Alsterdoff. Michalczewski later relinquished the cruiserweight crown to concentrate on the light-heavyweight championship. In so doing, he made the most consecutive successful defences of the title (a record of twenty-three) before losing the crown on 18 October 2003 against Julio Cesar Gonzalez of Mexico on points over twelve rounds at the Color Line Arena in Hamburg, Germany.

Jane Couch became the first female boxer to be licensed by the British Boxing Board of Control. Jane had her first professional contest on 30 October 1994, stopping Kalpna Shah in two rounds of a scheduled six in Wigan, Lancashire. Jane had a successful and colourful career, contributing a great deal to the cause of women's boxing during her time in the ring. Couch had her last contest on 8 December 2007 at the La Palestre in Le Cannet, France, against home fighter Anne Sophie Mathis, which resulted in a two-round stoppage defeat in a contest set for six. During her career, Jane took part in thirty-nine bouts (winning twenty-eight and losing eleven) after sharing the ring with many top fighters who were in action at the time.

George Foreman of America certainly shocked many boxing experts when he found the punch to dislodge defending WBA and IBF world heavyweight champion and fellow countryman Michael Moorer from the titles by a knockout in round ten of twelve. While Foreman was still a good fighter, there seemed no logical way that he could once again become king of the hill but in boxing, no boxer should be sold short, especially when that fighter is a known big puncher. That being said, Moorer looked in command in the early stages of the contest, frequently landing damaging blows to both the head and body of Foreman. The game-changing contest took place at the MGM Grand, Grand Garden Arena in Las Vegas on 5 November 1994. In defeating Moorer, Foreman not only regained the championship (he lost the undisputed title to Muhammad Ali on 30 October 1974 by a knockout in eight rounds of a scheduled fifteen at the Stade du 20 Mai in Kinshasa, Democratic Republic of the Congo), but he made history at the time by becoming at the age of forty-five years, nine months, and twenty-six days, the oldest man in the division to win a major version of the crown.

On 23 November 1994, Paul Weir became the first boxer from the UK to win a version of the world light-flyweight title when he outpointed South African Paul Oulden over twelve entertaining rounds at the Magnum Centre in Irvine, Scotland, to capture the vacant WBO crown. Weir also became the first Scottish boxer to win a world championship in two different weight divisions, having previously held the WBO World minimumweight title.

Chris Eubank was not a man who kept his title in cold storage. Eubank can claim the record of having defended the world super-middleweight title more often in any one year than any other champion in the division. The very active Eubank achieved this feat in 1994 by making six defences of the WBO championship.

Dennis Andries became the first former British light-heavyweight champion to win the domestic crown at cruiserweight in a contest that took place on 21 January 1995 when he crossed gloves with opponent Denzil Browne. The two fighters met at the Scottish Exhibition Centre in Glasgow. A determined Andries made it his night when he claimed the vacant title by way of a stoppage in round eleven of twelve.

On 22 February 1995, Richie Woodhall (the reigning Commonwealth middleweight title-holder) added the vacant European crown to his name when he stopped Italian Silvio Branco in round nine of a twelve round contest. The battle for the championship took place at the Ice Rink in Telford, Shropshire. The win over Branco proved to be a good name on Woodhall's record since on 10 October 2003, the Italian won the WBA world light-heavyweight title. Branco travelled to France and at the Palais des Sports, Marseille, unexpectedly defeated the defending champion, France's Mehdi Sahnoune, in the eleventh round of a twelve-round contest.

Above: George Foreman
(left), seen with promoter Jack
Solomons, regained the world
heavyweight championship in
1994. (*Derek Rowe*)

Left: Chris Eubank
defended his WBO world
super-middleweight title on six
occasions in 1994. (*Les Clark*)

At the London Arena, former world, British, European, Commonwealth welter, and Commonwealth super-welterweight champion Lloyd Honeyghan retired from his role as an active boxer. Honeyghan bowed out on 25 February 1995 when being stopped in round three of a slated ten-round contest. The defeat came at the hands of the then latest prospect: Adrian Dodson, a boxer who was undefeated in eleven professional outings. In his prime, Honeyghan was an outstanding fighter who would have been too much for his opponent Dodson to handle, but time moves on. During his career, the former champion had amassed a record of forty-eight fights (winning forty-three with just five defeats). Honeyghan had traded with a host of class fighters, nine having held a world championship during their careers: men like like Gianfranco Rosi (WBC and later IBF super-welterweight), Don Curry (undisputed welterweight and WBC super-welterweight), Johnny Bumphus (WBA super-lightweight), Maurice Blocker (WBC and later IBF welterweight), Gene Hatcher (WBC super-lightweight), Jorge Vaca (WBC welterweight), Marlon Starling (WBA and later WBC welterweight), Mark Breland (WBA welterweight), and Vinny Pazienza (IBF world lightweight and WBA super-welterweight)—indeed a most impressive list.

Ireland's Steve Collins is the only man in the professional ranks to have twice defeated both Chris Eubank and Nigel Benn. Collins won the WBO world super-middleweight crown when he outpointed Chris Eubank over twelve rounds on 18 March 1995 at Greens Glenn Arena in Millstreet, Ireland. The expert opinion before the contest was that Eubank would still be the reigning champion when the fight had concluded, so the outcome was somewhat of a shock when Collins took the crown and ended Eubank's undefeated record, which then stood at forty-one wins with two drawn. Collins hence made the first defence against Eubank on 9 September 1995 at the Pairc Ui Chaoimh in Cork, Ireland. Collins confirmed that his first victory over Eubank was no fluke and once again pleased the home fans by outpointing him over the duration of twelve rounds. On 6 July 1996, Collins made the fourth defence of the crown against the formidable former WBO world middleweight and WBC super-middleweight king Nigel Benn at the Nynex Arena in Manchester. This outing looked like a tough one for the Irishman, but Collins proved he was a worthy champion, successfully retained the title when Benn retired in round four of twelve. The pair had their second meeting in the ring on 9 November 1996 at the same venue; on this occasion, Collins defeated Benn when he retired in round six of a scheduled twelve.

The inaugural European title bout to be staged at super-bantamweight took place on 5 April 1995 between former European bantamweight king Vincenzo Belcastro of Italy and Sergey Devakov of Ukraine in Alassio,

Steve Collins twice defeated
Chris Eubank and Nigel
Benn in WBO world
super-middleweight title
fights. (*Les Clark*)

Italy. After twelve rounds of competitive boxing, Belcastro had his arm lifted in victory and hence became the first champion at the weight when he took the title with a twelve-round points decision.

On 23 May 1995, Michael Ayers stepped out to defend his British lightweight championship against Charles Shepherd at the Furzefield Leisure Centre, Hertfordshire. It was a successful night for Ayers as he retained his crown by a stoppage in the third stanza of a scheduled twelve-round encounter. Ayers thus became the quickest title-holder in the division at the time to win a Lonsdale Belt outright: a period of three months and six days. Ayers first won the vacant domestic title on 17 February 1995 when in a championship set for twelve rounds, he defeated opponent Paul Burke by a stoppage in round six. That fight took place at the Leisure Centre in Crawley, Sussex. The first defence for Ayers took place very quickly; the following month, on 31 March 1995 at the National Sports Centre in Crystal Palace, London, challenger Karl Taylor was stopped in the eighth of a scheduled twelve-round encounter.

Japan witnessed one of their champions being dethroned on 30 July 1995 when Northern Ireland's Wayne McCullough challenged title-holder

Yasuei Yakushiji for the WBC world bantamweight crown. The odds were stacked heavily against McCullough, who was up against a worthy title-holder who was making the fifth defence of his championship. The Irish boxer duly pulled out all the stops and at the end of the scheduled twelve-round contest, which was staged at the Aichi Prefectural Gym in Nagoya, the challenger was given the decision on points. On this occasion, McCullough became the first fighter from the British Isles to capture a world title in this country.

Veeraphol Sahaprom of Thailand won the WBA world bantamweight title on 17 September 1995, defeating holder and fellow countryman Daorung Chuwatana by a twelve-round points decision. In so doing, Sahapron won the title in just his fourth professional contest. The bout took place in Nonthaburi, Thailand.

Shinji Takehara won the WBA world middleweight championship on 19 December 1995 at the Korakuen Hall in Tokyo, Japan, outpointing defending title-holder Jorge Castro of Argentina over twelve rounds. Takehara thus became the first Japanese boxer to win a world crown in this weight division.

The spectators hardly had time to catch their breath, let alone settle into their seats, when Bernard Hopkins defended his IBF world middleweight title on 27 January 1996 at the Veteran's Memorial Coliseum in Phoenix, Arizona. Hopkins went to work, quickly landing his punches on target to retain his crown in twenty-four seconds of the first round against Guyana-born Steve Frank, making it the second fastest win in a world middleweight title contest at that time.

The reigning IBF world light-heavyweight king Henry Maske of Germany made the ninth defence of his title on 17 February 1986 against Jamaican-born Duran Williams at the Arena Westfalenhalle in Dortmund, Germany. Maske put on a competent display of boxing in front of his home fans against a worthy challenger to retain his title by way of a twelve-round points decision. Maske had won a gold medal at the 1988 Olympic Games, which had taken place in South Korea. Maske captured the respective medal at middleweight, defeating Canada's Egerton Marcus. Maske eventually turned his attention to the 'punch for pay' ranks and made his professional debut on the 9 May 1990, not in Germany but in the UK at the Grand Hall in Wembley, London. Maske was impressive and made short work of his opponent Antonio Arvizu, knocking him out in round one of a scheduled six.

On 16 March 1996, England's Naseem Hamed defended his WBO world featherweight title against challenger Said Lawal of Nigeria at the Scottish Exhibition Centre in Glasgow. Hamed was expected to retain his championship without experiencing any kind of problems from his

Henry Maske started his
professional career in the UK.
(*Les Clark*)

challenger. A win inside the distance looked more than likely for the
defending champion. Yet few if any pundits expected Hamed to dispatch
Lawal as quickly as he did. Hamed was in no mood to hang around in the
ring on the night and retained his crown in double quick time stopping
Lawal in thirty-five seconds of the first round. On this occasion, Hamed
put his name in the record books by scoring the fastest ever win in a world
featherweight title bout at that time.

On 13 April 1996, Uzbekistan-born Artur Grigorian met former IBF
world featherweight champion Antonio Rivera of Puerto Rico at the
Sporthalle Wandsber in Hamburg, Germany, for the vacant WBO version
of the world lightweight crown. Grigorian secured the crown when he
knocked out his challenger in round twelve. Grigorian remained champion
until 3 January 2004 when Acelino Freitas of Brazil relieved him of the
title at the Foxwoods Resort in Mashantucket, Connecticut, scoring a
twelve-round points decision. However, during his reign as champion,
Grigorian created a record by defending the title successfully more often
than any other previous title-holder in the division, the total number of
defences made being seventeen in all.

Robbie Regan showed his impressive boxing ability by winning the WBO
world bantamweight championship on 26 April 1996. Regan outpointed

Naseem Hamed dispatched his challenger, Said Lawal, in record-breaking time in 1996 when defending his WBO world featherweight title. (*Les Clark*)

defending title-holder Daniel Jimenez of Puerto Rico over twelve rounds in an exciting match. The bout took place at the Welsh Institute of Sport in Cardiff. On this occasion, Regan became the first Welsh boxer to capture a world crown in this division.

On 29 June 1996, Alexander Zaitsev won the vacant European middleweight title by ending the contribution to the contest of Italy's Agostino Cardamone by a knockout in round ten of a bout set for twelve. The meeting between the two fighters took place at Sassari Sardegna in Italy. By capturing this championship, Zaitsev became the first Russian to win a European crown.

On 20 September 1996, middleweight Robbie Sims had his final professional contest outpointing opponent Jose Burgos over eight rounds at the Bayside Expo Center in Boston, Massachusetts. Sims finished with a record of fifty bouts (winning thirty-eight, losing ten, and drawing two). While this was an impressive tally, Sims had an impossible act to follow when it came to living up to his half-brother since he was none other than former world middleweight champion Marvin Hagler, a man considered to be one of the greats in the division.

Richie Woodhall (the then European and Commonwealth middleweight champion) made his American debut on 19 October 1996 at the Show Place

Above: Robbie Regan (right) defeats Daniel Jimenez to win the WBO world bantamweight crown in 1996. (*Les Clark*)

Left: Robbie Regan holds up his world championship belt after his victory over Jimenez. (*Les Clark*)

Arena in Upper Marlboro, Maryland. The outing for Woodhall was the big one—a crack at the WBC world middleweight crown held by Keith Holmes, who would be making the first defence of the title. Holmes was parading his wares in front of his home fans; he had every intention of looking good and keeping his name on the championship belt. Holmes's record was thirty fights (twenty-nine wins with one defeat) while Woodhall was undefeated in twenty-one bouts. There was no disputing that Woodhall was faced with a difficult task and while victory was not beyond him, the likelihood of one was truthfully low. This pessimistic view proved to be true when the Briton was stopped in the twelfth and final round. This was not the end for Woodhall's world title aspirations as after one more winning bout, he was back once again challenging for a world championship this time at the higher weight division super-middleweight. On 27 March 1988 at the Ice Rink, Woodhall boxed his way to a twelve-round points decision to take the WBC world super-middleweight title from South African holder Thulani Malinga.

The undefeated Pele Reid was getting the reputation as a hard-punching heavyweight who took his man out early during a contest by a knockout or a stoppage. Reid had won all his previous seven fights inside the distance, five victories coming inside the opening session. It could therefore be said that at the Hillsborough Leisure Centre in Sheffield on 25 February 1997, no one felt that his bout with fellow Briton Michael Murray (who had gained victory in fifteen of his twenty-seven paid outings) would go the full distance of eight rounds. The view was that Reid would have another early night. This proved to be more than true when Reid once again in the first round halted Murray in just nine seconds, thus creating a record at the time of being the fastest win seen inside a British ring. However, in all fairness to Murray, it has to be said that he was not defeated by the power of Reid's punching but by a dislocated shoulder that made it impossible for him to carry on in this contest.

During 1997, Tania Follett scored a knockout blow for the role of women's involvement in the noble art, when she etched her name into the record books by becoming Britain's first female boxing manager. Tania had previously made her mark in boxing by becoming the first UK corner woman; now she had scored the double.

On 14 March 1997, Ryan Rhodes retained his British super-welterweight title against challenger and former two-time British welterweight champion Del Bryan by a seven-round stoppage in a contest set for twelve at the Rivermead Leisure Centre in Reading, Berkshire. Rhodes was on top of his game and at that particular time, he created a record by winning the Lonsdale Belt outright in the fastest time: a period of ninety days. Ryan had won the vacant crown on 14 December 1996, impressively stopping former WBO world super-welterweight king Paul Jones in eight rounds of

High-kicking heavyweight Pele Reid secured the fastest win in a British ring in 1997. (*Les Clark*)

twelve at the Ponds Forge Arena in Sheffield, Yorkshire. Rhodes followed this by a first successful defence against Peter Waudy on 25 February 1997 at the Hillsborough Leisure Centre in Sheffield when knocking his challenger in the first round of a scheduled twelve.

It appeared only a matter of time before the UK would produce its first European champion in the super-bantamweight division. The man to take that honour was Spencer Oliver on 20 May 1997 at the Pickett's Lock Stadium in Edmonton, London. The defending title-holder sharing the ring with Oliver was Martin Krastev of Bulgaria, who became an ex-champion when stopped in round four of a contest set for twelve.

On 11 September 1997, Hacine Cherifi of France failed in his challenge for the WBC world super-middleweight crown at the Kingsway Leisure Centre in Widnes, Cheshire, when outpointed over twelve rounds by Britain's defending champion Robin Reid. However, it was not all over for Cherifi regarding the world title. The Frenchman bounced back from this defeat when in his very next fight, which took place on 2 May 1998, he entered the fray once again and challenged the WBC world middleweight champion, Keith Holmes of America, at the Astroballe in Villeurbanne, France. Based on the two fighters' respective records, the likely outcome

Ryan Rhodes pictured
wearing the WBC
international champion's
belt won the Lonsdale
Belt in quick time in 1997.
(*Philip Sharkey*)

was a victory for the American. However, the Frenchman provided a
minor shock and was successful in his bid for the crown when he won a
twelve-round points decision to take the title.

Herbie Hide wasted no time in disposing of his challenger when
defending his WBO world heavyweight crown on 18 April 1998. The fans
in attendance had no fears of missing the last train or bus home. Hide
hence registered the fastest win in a world heavyweight title fight when
he stopped American opponent Damon Reed in fifty-two seconds of the
first round. This record-making feat by the British fighter took place at the
Nynex Arena, Manchester. The contest was scheduled for twelve rounds.

Chris Eubank attempted for the second time to win a third world title
on 18 July 1998 at the Sheffield Arena in Yorkshire. Eubank, the former
WBO world middleweight and super-middleweight world champion,
was going up against the defending WBO world cruiserweight king Carl
Thompson, a fellow Briton. In a previous attempt at this title, Eubank
lost a twelve-round points decision at the Nynex Arena, Manchester, on
18 April 1988. Once again, Eubank failed to lift the crown when he had
to retire in round nine of twelve due to a badly swollen left eye. This was
the first time that Eubank had been halted inside the scheduled distance

in the professional ranks. During his career, Eubank had participated in fifty-two fights (winning forty-five, losing five, and drawing two). Eubank shared the ring with a host of quality opposition who had at one time or another held a version of a world championship: Nigel Benn (WBO middleweight and WBC super-middleweight), Thulani Malinga (WBC super-middleweight), Lindell Holmes (IBF super-middleweight), Graciano Rocchigiani (IBF super-middleweight and (WBC light-heavyweight), Steve Collins (WBO middleweight and super-middleweight), Joe Calzaghe (WBO, IBF, WBC, and WBA super-middleweight), and Carl Thompson. At the time of his departure from trading punches in the ring, Eubank held the record of going the distance of twelve rounds in world super-middleweight title bouts more often than any other fighter at that time (be it in the role of champion or challenger), the total being fifteen.

Harry Simon became the first boxer from Namibia to win a world title when he outpointed American Ronald Wright over twelve rounds to capture the WBO super-welterweight crown. The contest took place at the Carousel Casino in Hammanskraal, South Africa, on 22 August 1998.

On 30 November 1998, American Terry Norris failed to win the WBA version of the world super-welterweight crown when French holder Laurent Boudouani stopped him in round nine of twelve to retain the championship. The contest, which took place at the Palais des Sports in Paris, proved to be the last professional contest that Norris was to participate in. However, Norris left the sport with a record of forty-seven wins and nine defeats and at the time had taken part in more world title bouts in the division than any other boxer, the total being twenty-five of which he won nineteen. During his period in the paid ranks, he held both the WBC and IBF versions of the world championship. Norris was also the first fighter at the poundage to capture the crown on three separate occasions.

Judith Rollstone was appointed the first female administrative steward at the British Boxing Board of Control in 1998. At the time, Judith was a commercial solicitor in London. Mary Peters MBE was already an honorary steward but unlike Judith, she had no role in the decision process.

Lennox Lewis of the UK became a unified world heavyweight champion on 13 November 1999 when at the Thomas and Mack Centre, Las Vegas, he outpointed American Evander Holyfield over twelve tough rounds. Coming into the contest, Lewis was the WBC ruler with Holyfield holding both the IBF and WBA crowns. In this contest, the vacant IBO championship was also at stake. This was the second meeting between the two fighters; their first unification battle took place on 13 March 1999 at Madison Square Garden in New York. On that occasion, the contest once again went the full twelve rounds and was declared a draw.

9

Round Nine: 2000–2010

On 26 April 2000, J'Marie Moore had her second and last winning professional contest in the heavyweight division, stopping fellow American Anita Wells in the third session of a scheduled four-round contest. The bout took place in New Orleans, Louisiana. J'Marie was the daughter of a former world light-heavyweight champion, a fighter who is considered to be one of the greats in boxing: Archie Moore.

Felix Savon of Cuba became the third boxer to win three consecutive gold medals at the Olympic Games. Heavyweight Savon achieved this feat at the 2000 Games, which took place in Sydney, Australia, when he outpointed Sultan Ibragimov of Russia. Previously, Savon took gold at the 1992 Games, outpointing David Izonritei of Nigeria in Barcelona, Spain. The Cuban fighter then acquired his second gold medal in 1996 in Atlanta, outpointing David Defiabon of Canada to take his place on top of the podium.

Many sportsmen had been knighted over the years for their services to their respected sport. However, it was noticeable that not one boxer had received the honour. That trend was duly broken in 2000 when former British, European, and Commonwealth heavyweight champion Henry Cooper became the first from the sport to be knighted. Cooper, who was affectionately known as 'our Enry', hence became Sir Henry Cooper, who had been a credit to boxing during his time in the ring. Henry had previously been awarded an OBE in 1969.

On 28 April 2001, Germany's Mario Veit stepped between the ropes at the International Arena in Cardiff, Wales, to challenge Welsh holder Joe Calzaghe for the WBO world super-middleweight title. The two fighters had an identical record, being undefeated in thirty bouts. However, Joe,

Henry Cooper became the first boxer in 2000 to receive a knighthood. (*Derek Rowe*)

who was a class above his challenger, took away his undefeated status in no uncertain manner, stopping him in the opening round of twelve. In so doing, Calzaghe achieved at that time the fastest win in a world championship bout in the division, the stoppage over Veit taking place in a time of 112 seconds.

An intriguing contest took place on 8 June 2001 when the daughters of two great world heavyweight champions stepped into the ring to swap punches at the Turning Stone Resort and Casino Verona in New York. Laila Ali (daughter of Muhammad Ali) and Jacqui Frazier-Lyde (daughter of Joe Frazier) were both undefeated in their professional careers—Laila with nine bouts and Jacqui with seven. The fight created a great deal of interest, mostly due to their legendary fathers. At the end of the bout, Ali continued her undefeated run, winning on points over eight rounds. The bout may not have come up to the standards of the three bouts in which their legendary fathers once took part, but their fight nevertheless was entertaining with both boxers not holding back in the encounter.

On 29 September 2001, Ricardo Lopez of Mexico made a successful defence of his IBF world light-flyweight title when he impressively knocked out South African challenger Zolani Petelo of South Africa in round eight

Laila Ali (daughter of
Muhammad Ali) met Jacqui
Frazier-Lyde (daughter of Joe
Frazier) in a contest during
2001. (*Les Clark*)

in a scheduled twelve at Madison Square Garden in New York. After this
bout, Lopez announced his retirement from the sport he served so well.
Lopez was leaving the ring with a record of fifty-two fights (winning fifty-
one with one technical draw). The Mexican had also won the WBO, WBC,
and WBA versions of the world minimumweight titles during his career.
Lopez also captured the IBF world light-flyweight crown. During his career,
Lopez had participated in twenty-three world minimumweight title bouts
and three IBF light-flyweight title contests. Lopez's name truly belongs on
the list of greats in boxing. Also departing from boxing that night was
another great: the wellrespected American referee Arthur Mercante Sr,
who handled the contest and showed that age was no hindrance to him
carrying out his job at the incredible age of eighty-one years, eight months,
and three days. However, he too later announced his retirement from the
sport he had also served so well.

Harry Simon entered the ring on 6 April 2002 to challenge Sweden's
Armand Krajnc for the WBO world middleweight championship. The
contest at the Cirkusbygningen in Copenhagen, Denmark, went the full
twelve-round distance, at the end of which the title changed hands. Simon
not only became the new champion but also the first fighter from Namibia

to win a world title in two different weight divisions. Simon was a former holder of the WBO world super-welterweight title.

At the Provincial Gymnasium in Khon Kaen, Thailand, on 19 April 2002, defending WBC world flyweight champion Pongsaklek Wonjongkam retained his crown successfully on home ground when he knocked out challenger Daisuke Naito of Japan. Wonjongkam's fans did not see him in the ring for very long since he took his man out of the fight in the first round of twelve. Wonjongkam obviously did not wish to linger any longer than he need do. In so doing, he registered the fastest win in the division at that particular time: the bout was concluded in thirty-four seconds.

On 18 May 2002, Naseem Hamed had his last professional contest at the London Arena in Millwall, London. The British fighter, who had brought a great deal of excitement to the sport during his career, outpointed Spaniard Manuel Calvo, a former European title-holder, over twelve rounds. In this meeting, Hamed won the vacant IBO version of the world featherweight crown. The bout failed to sparkle in any way whatsoever and was a far cry from Naseem's previous spectacular performances. Along with the IBO title, Hamed had won the WBO, IBF, and WBC world featherweight championships during his career. At bantamweight, Naseem acquired the European bantamweight title along with the WBC international super-bantamweight crown. In a total of thirty-seven paid bouts, Hamed lost just once and that was on a twelve-round points decision to Mexican Marco Antonio Barrera on 7 April 2001 at the MGM Grand in Las Vegas during a bout for the vacant IBO title. The defeat against Barrera was in no way a disgrace since he was an exceptional fighter. Prior to this contest, many tipped the Briton to win, which spoke volumes for the abilities of Naseem.

Hamed fought eleven men who had at one time or another held a world title during their careers inside the ring; these fighters were Juan Polo Perez, (IBF super-flyweight), Steve Robinson (WBO featherweight), Manuel Medina (IBF, WBC, and WBO featherweight), Tom Johnson (IBF featherweight), Kevin Kelley (WBC featherweight), Wilfredo Vazquez (WBA featherweight, bantamweight, and super-bantamweight), Wayne McCullough (WBC bantamweight), Paul Ingle (IBF featherweight), Cesar Soto (WBC featherweight), Vuyani Bungu (IBF super-bantamweight), and Marco Antonio Barrera (WBO and WBC super-bantamweight, WBC featherweight, and WBC and IBF super-featherweight). Nassem was inducted into the International Hall of Fame in 2015.

On 22 May 2002, Irichelle Duran of Panama, who boxed in the super-bantamweight division, had her third and last professional contest when she lost a four-round points decision to American Angie Bordelon at the Alario Center in Westwego, Louisiana. During her respective career,

Irichelle only won one of her three bouts; that victory came in her second contest when she stopped Marilyn Hernandez of the Dominion Republic in the third round of four on 5 October 2000 at the Magnum Events in Panama City. Her father was the great Roberto Duran.

Panama's Guillermo Jones came to the UK on 23 November 2002 to challenge England's Johnny Nelson for the WBO world cruiserweight title at the Derby Storm Arena. Jones made the most of his opportunity and pushed Nelson hard throughout the fight. Jones had not come to the UK just to make up the numbers; he wanted that world title. However, after twelve rounds of boxing, the contest was declared a draw, hence Nelson retained the crown. Jones did not lose heart by the result. On 27 September 2008, he once again stepped into the ring to challenge for a world crown, this time for the WBA version of the championship at the Color Line Arena in Altona, Hamburg. Jones was again fighting in the defending champion's backyard, crossing gloves with title-holder Firat Arslan. In this challenge, Jones did not rely on the judge's scorecards, hence his bid proved successful when he stopped the defending champion in round ten of twelve.

Scott Harrison became the first Scottish fighter to regain a world title in the paid ranks on 29 November 2003, stopping defending WBO featherweight king Manuel Medina of Mexico in round eleven of a contest scheduled for twelve. Harrison first won the title on 19 October 2002 outpointing holder Julio Pablo Chacon of Argentina over twelve rounds. Harrison had hence lost the championship in his second defence to Medina, suffering a twelve-round points defence on 12 July 2003. All three of the bouts took place at the Braehead Arena in Glasgow, Scotland.

Germany's Sven Ottke gave his home fans plenty to celebrate on 27 March 2004 when he turned back the challenge of former WBO world middleweight king Armand Krajnc of Sweden for his WBA and IBF world super-middleweight titles. The contest took place at the Bordelandhalle in Magdeburg, Germany. After this bout, Ottke retired from the sport with an undefeated record of thirty-four bouts, having made twenty-one consecutive defences of the title (then a record for the weight division).

On 16 April 2004, Roberto Duran Jr, who boxed at welterweight level, had his last professional contest when outpointed by fellow Panamanian Nicasio Sanchez over four rounds at the Figali Convention Centre in Fort Amador, Panama. During his career, Duran Jr took part in seven paid bouts (winning five, losing one, with one no contest). Roberto had a difficult task attempting to emulate his father's success in the ring. His father was the great Roberto Duran.

In a unification bout on 18 September 2004, Bernard Hopkins (the WBC, WBA, and IBF holder) met fellow American and WBO champion

Oscar De La Hoya at the MGM Grand in Las Vegas. The meeting between the two fighters was one that was greatly anticipated by fight followers. Hopkins emerged victorious and became the first undisputed world middleweight champion since 1980 when he knocked out De La Hoya in round nine. Prior to this contest, the last undisputed world middleweight champion was Marvin Hagler.

It was success at last for Britain's Clinton Woods, who finally won a major version of the world light-heavyweight title when he stopped American Rico Hoye at the Magna Centre in Rotherham, Yorkshire, on 4 March 2005. The contest saw Woods punch his way to a stoppage in the fifth session in a bout scheduled for twelve rounds to claim the vacant IBF crown. This was Woods's fourth attempt at winning the championship at the poundage. Woods had his first crack at the championship on 7 September 2002 against a man considered to be a modern-day great: Roy Jones Jr, who was the undisputed champion holding the WBA, WBC, IBF, IBO, IBA, and WBF versions of the title. Fight experts did not give Woods any kind of chance of winning the title against this man; they were proven to be correct when the Briton, while putting up a brave bid, was not able to compete with the champion, being soundly outboxed before being stopped. The referee hence wisely decided to bring the bout to a close in round six of a bout set for twelve. The bout had taken place at the Rose Garden in Portland, Oregon. A second chance arose for Woods when he was matched with Jamaican-born Glen Johnson at the Hillsborough Leisure Centre in Sheffield, Yorkshire, on 7 November 2003 for the vacant IBF crown. While being a good fighter, Johnson was no Roy Jones Jr, so the task for Woods looked like being a good deal easier and a victory for him seemed more than possible. At the end of a hard-fought twelve-round bout, the fight was declared a draw so once again, Woods failed to secure a world crown. A rematch between the pair took place on 6 February 2004 at the Ponds Forge Arena in Sheffield; hopes were high that a British win would light up the home fans. The bout went the full distance of twelve rounds, at the end of which a winner was found and a new champion was crowned. Sadly for UK fans, it was not Woods but Johnson who took the decision and the championship. At that moment, it looked as if the British fighter's hopes of ever becoming a world champion were dashed forever. However, Woods did not lose heart and fought on; he eventually achieved his dream when meeting Hoye.

American super-welterweight Tyrone Brunson made his professional debut on 22 April 2005 at the Blue Horizon in Philadelphia, Pennsylvania, against fellow countryman Kevin Carey, who he stopped in round one of four. Brunson acquired a reputation for being a powerful puncher with the habit of winning in the opening round. Brunson was knocking down his

Clinton Woods on his fourth attempt won a version of the world light-heavyweight title in 2005. (*Les Clark*)

opponents like nine pins in quick time. However, the first-round victories could not go on indefinitely and his trend of quick victories came to an end on 15 August 2008 when Antonio Soriano of Mexico held him to a draw over six rounds at The Venue at River Cree in Alberta, Canada. Prior to the Soriano bout, Brunson attained the record of winning more consecutive bouts in the first round at that time than any other fighter the number: nineteen in total.

England's Ricky Hatton gave boxing in the UK a tremendous boost when he pulled off a magnificent victory on 4 June 2005, winning the IBF super-lightweight title. While many fancied Hatton to win, the outcome was far from certain against such a well-schooled and experienced fighter. The challenger, however, put in an outstanding performance to stop the highly regarded Russian-born Australian world champion, Kostya Tszyu. The defending title-holder found Hatton's relentless pressure too much to handle and he hence surrendered his crown, retiring in round eleven of a contest scheduled for twelve at the M.E.N. Arena.

In the inaugural contest for the Women's WBC world flyweight title, England's Cathy Brown and Italy's Stefania Bianchini gloved up on 7 August 2005 to do battle to find the first-ever champion at the weight. The two women battled away earnestly at the Palaflaminio Rimini in Emilia-

Ricky Hatton secured a magnificent win in 2005 by winning the IBF world super-lightweight title. (*Les Clark*)

Romagna, Italy, showing impressive skills. When the fight concluded, a new champion was crowned in the shape of Bianchini, who was awarded the ten-round points decision.

On 16 September 2005, Scott Dann retained his British middleweight crown when he outpointed challenger Wayne Elcock over twelve rounds at the Pavilions in Plymouth, Devon. This was a historical occasion since it was the first British title bout to have three judges officiate; they were Mark Green, Terry O'Connor, and Richard Davies.

On 16 September 2005, Eliza Olson won the WBC world female lightweight title and the IBA crown when she outpointed holder Jessica Rakoczy of Canada over ten rounds at the Palace Indian Gaming Centre in Lemoore, California. Eliza's grandfather would have been more than proud of her achievement on this day since he was the former world middleweight champion Carl Bobo Olson.

In his last professional contest, England's Johnny Nelson retained his WBO world cruiserweight title on 26 November 2005 for the thirteenth time, outpointing Italian challenger Vincenzo Cantatore over twelve rounds. The contest, which took place at the Palazzetto dello Sport in

Rome, Italy, saw Nelson create a record at that time of making more title defences in the division than any other champion.

On 17 December 2005, Russian Nikolay Valuev outpointed American holder John Ruiz over twelve rounds to capture the WBA world heavyweight crown at the Max-Schmeling-Halle in Berlin, Germany. In so doing, he became the tallest man at the recorded height of 7 feet (some records have him at 7 feet 2 inches) to hold a version of the championship. Valuev was a true giant among the giants in the world of heavyweight boxing title-holders. In contrast, on 23 February 1906, Canadian Tommy Burns outpointed defending champion Marvin Hart of American over twenty rounds at the Pacific AC in Los Angeles, California, to win the heavyweight title. On that occasion, Burns became, at the recorded height of 5 feet 7 inches, the shortest man to hold the championship.

On 4 March 2006, Joe Calzaghe from Wales (the WBO world super-middleweight title-holder) met American IBF world champion Jeff Lacy in a unification contest at the M.E.N. Arena. Calzaghe was making the eighteenth defence of his crown and going into battle with an undefeated record of forty bouts. Lacy would be making his fifth defence of his title

Nikolay Valuev, the tallest man (at the reported height of 7 feet and 2 inches) to hold a version of the world heavyweight title.
(*Les Clark*)

and was also undefeated in twenty-two contests with one no decision. This was a bout many boxing experts felt the Welshman would lose for Lacy was considered the number one man in the division—a force to be reckoned with, a new star in boxing. Once again, boxing showed that shocks continue to take place and the only certain thing in the sport is its uncertainty. Calzaghe turned in a most outstanding performance; he not only schooled the American but completely outclassed him and took the verdict on points over the duration of twelve rounds. It was, in truth, amazing that the American was able to last the full distance. Joe was now looked upon as someone a little special.

Venezuelan Edwin Valero entered the ring on 5 August 2006 at the Figali Convention Center, Panama City to challenge home fighter and defending WBA world super-featherweight champion Vicente Mosquera. Valero was undefeated in nineteen professional bouts, amazingly winning eighteen of them in the opening round—testament indeed to his punching ability. Mosquera also had a good record, having taken part in twenty-six bouts (winning twenty-four, losing one, and drawing one). Valero took the crown when he stopped Mosquera in round ten of a scheduled twelve-round battle. After four defences of the world super-featherweight title, Valero relinquished the crown and moved up a weight division. On 4 April 2009, he contested the vacant WBC world lightweight championship against Mexican-born Antonio Pitalua at the Frank Erwin Center in Austin, Texas, and the hard-punching fighting machine became a title-holder once again when the fight was stopped in his favour in the second session of a scheduled twelve. Valero looked to be on the road to ring greatness; such was the manner of his victories and bigger fights loomed on the horizon. However, life often takes a turn few can see coming. Valero had his last contest on 6 February 2010 when he defeated Mexican Antonio De Marco in the second defence of his world lightweight crown at the Arena Monterry in Nuevo León, Mexico. De Marco retired in the ninth session of a bout scheduled for twelve. During his career in the paid ranks, Valero won all his twenty-seven bouts inside the distance. Tragically, Valero committed suicide in 2010 while in a jail cell after being arrested on suspicion of killing his wife.

Cathy Brown won the vacant women's English bantamweight title on 24 September 2006 at the York Hall in Bethnal Green, London, when she outpointed opponent Juliette Winter over ten rounds. In so doing, Cathy went into the contest with a record of twenty bouts with twelve victories and eight defeats; she became the first woman to hold this championship. In defeating Winter, Cathy also avenged a four-round points defeat that she had suffered on 20 March 2003 at the Porchester Hall in Queensway, London. During her career, Brown also held the WIBF version of the European flyweight championship.

Cathy Brown, the first holder of the women's English bantamweight title in 2006. (*Les Clark*)

It was a fight that promised much and it delivered in every way. The two men considered to be the very best in their weight division met in a showdown at the Millennium Stadium in Cardiff, Wales, on 3 November 2007. The contest was a unification fight between the WBO holder Joe Calzaghe from Wales and rival champion Mikkel Kessler from Denmark, who was the WBC and WBA world super-middleweight champion. The pair were undefeated: Calzaghe in forty-three bouts and Kessler in thirty-nine outings. The contest went the full route of twelve rounds and at the end, the points decision went to the Welshman. On defeating Kessler, Calzaghe acquired the distinction of being the first boxer to have held the four major versions of the title at the poundage at one time or another, these being the WBO, IBF, WBC, and WBA.

Chris Edwards went into the record books when he became the first man to hold the British super-flyweight crown. Edwards achieved this honour when he outpointed opponent Jamie McDonnell over twelve rounds in a contest for the inaugural title on 8 December 2007 at the Robin Park Centre in Wigan, Lancashire.

Frankie Gavin well and truly put his name in the history books when he became the first English boxer to win a world amateur championship in Chicago. Frankie won the gold medal when he put in a fine performance to defeat Italian Domenico Valentino 19–10 at lightweight during 2007.

On 14 March 2008, David Barnes won the vacant British super-lightweight title when he outpointed former European super-lightweight champion Ted Bami over the course of twelve rounds. The venue for the contest was the George Carnall Leisure Centre in Davyhulme, Manchester. On this occasion, Barnes acquired the distinction of being the first former British welterweight champion to move down a division and capture this crown. Barnes reigned has British welter champion from 2003 to 2005.

Mexican Manuel Medina engaged in his last professional contest on 29 August 2008 at the Carousel Casino in Hammanskraal North West, South Africa, against former IBF world super-featherweight king Malcolm Klassen, who was fighting on home turf. The contest was an IBF super-featherweight eliminator and one that saw Medina stopped in two rounds of twelve by his opponent. While Klassen was a talented ring operator who did all that was asked of him in the contest, it was obvious that the Mexican was not the fighter he once was; his timing of punch and indeed durability was now questionable. Time and hard fights against a long list of demanding opposition had taken its toll. During his career in the paid ranks, Medina proved to be an outstanding fighter, taking part in eighty-four bouts (winning sixty-seven, losing sixteen, and drawing one). Medina also has the distinction of being the only man to win a version of the world featherweight title on five separate occasions—a most remarkable feat.

The first championship win came on 12 August 1991. Medina put in a fine performance to take the IBF crown at the Great Western Forum in Inglewood, California, outpointing defending champion Troy Dorsey of America over twelve hard-fought rounds. For a time, Medina looked to be an exceptional title-holder. However, his reign came to an end when he lost the crown in his fifth defence, being outpointed by American Tom Johnson over the scheduled twelve-round distance. The contest against Johnson took place on 26 February 1993 at the Salle de Fetes in Melun, France. Medina revealed that he was still a man to contend with when he took his place on the champion's throne, once again winning the WBC version of the title. To achieve this, Medina outpointed fellow Mexican defending champion Alejandro Gonzalez over twelve sessions. The battle between the two respective fighters took place at the Convention Center in Sacramento, California, on 23 September 1995. Medina did not wear the WBC belt for a long since he became an ex-champion in his first defence. Challenger Luisito Espinosa of the Philippines boxed his way to the title, being awarded a twelve-round points decision over Medina at the Korayuen Hall in Tokyo, Japan, on 11 December 1995. At the San Jose Arena in California, Medina found himself king of the hill once again when he toppled the then champion and fellow countryman Hector Lizarraga, gaining a twelve-round points decision to take the IBF crown on 24 April 1998.

A visit to Britain in his second defence on 13 November 1999 saw Medina go head-to-head with home fighter Paul Ingle at the KC Sports Arena in Cottingham, Hull. It did not go well for the Mexican since he came out on the wrong side of the points decision after twelve bruising rounds. Medina was not finished yet when it came to world titles in the division. On 16 November 2001, champion Frankie Toledo of America was stopped in round five of twelve when putting his IBF belt on the line against his challenger at the Orleans Hotel and Casino, Las Vegas. Medina found disappointment in his first defence of the championship on 27 April 2002 when going up against former WBO and IBF world super-flyweight and WBO and WBA world bantamweight king Johnny Tapia of America at Madison Square Garden in New York. Tapia was a tough opponent and it was not exactly a shock when Medina came up short on the scorecards after twelve rounds and left the ring an ex-champion. The reigning WBO champion Scott Harrison gave Medina a shot at his title at Braehead Arena in Glasgow, Scotland, on 12 July 2003. Once again, the Mexican shocked those who had written him off and found himself with a world title when given a twelve-round points decision. Medina travelled back to the same venue on 29 November 2003 to face Harrison in a return bout, but this time, the Scot proved the superior fighter, regaining the title with a stoppage in round eleven of twelve. This was the last time that Medina would battle for a world featherweight crown.

The contest against Columbian Breidis Prescott proved to be a disaster on 6 September 2008 for England's Amir Khan. The two fighters entered the ring with almost identical records, both being undefeated: Khan in eighteen professional bouts and Prescott in nineteen visits to the ring. It clearly was not a fight that could be considered an easy outing for Khan. Prescott had not arrived on UK shores just to be a stepping stone for Khan; he was serious opposition who had his own very high ambitions in the sport. Khan was defending his WBO intercontinental lightweight crown in a contest scheduled for twelve rounds. It appeared that Amir, who looked headed for a world title shot, would emerge victorious with a successful defence of his title and continue his climb towards the top once the proceedings eventually came to a close. However, in boxing, it is risky to take anything for granted, especially when two ambitious undefeated fighters meet. This fight was an example of such a fact. A shock took place when Prescott knocked out Khan in the opening round; it had to be said that was not in the script.

A unique situation took place on 11 October 2008 when former WBC and WBO world heavyweight king Vitali Klitschko came out of retirement to challenge the then WBC champion Samuel Peter of Nigeria for the crown. It was no great surprise to the students of the sport when at the 02

World Arena in Berlin, Germany, a Klitschko victory was achieved. The man from Ukraine, despite being out of the ring for some time, showed that his absence from the sport had not blunted his fighting ability in any way whatsoever—a fact Peters was painfully aware of while the bout lasted. Peter retired in round eight of twelve after being outclassed throughout the contest. For the first time in the history of boxing, two brothers simultaneously held a version of a championship in this division as younger brother Wladimir was the IBF, WBO, and IBO title-holder.

On 31 October 2008, England's Don Broadhurst ensured that his name would go into the record books when he became the first holder of the Commonwealth super-flyweight title by outpointing Ghana's Isaac Quaye over twelve rounds for the vacant crown at the Aston Villa Leisure Centre in Birmingham.

At the Nottingham Arena in Nottingham, on 6 December 2008, England's Carl Froch won the vacant WBC world super-middleweight crown when he outpointed Canada's Jean Pascal over twelve tough and rugged rounds. It was not an easy night for Carl, who had to fight hard against his opponent but he deserved his well-earned victory against a competitive opponent. This was not the end for Pascal's world title ambitions for in his second bout after his defeat to Froch, he more than proved his quality when he challenged for the WBC world light-heavyweight crown on 19 June 2009. The bid took place at the Bell Centre in Montreal, Canada; it was successful for Pascal as after twelve rounds of boxing, he claimed the crown when he outpointed Romanian-born defending champion Adrian Diaconu.

Former two-time former WBA world super-welterweight champion Julio Cesar Vasquez paid his last professional visit to the ring at the Club Atletico Sarmiento in Buenos Aires, Argentina, on 19 June 2009 against fellow Argentinian Silvio Walter Rojas. The contest resulted in a draw after four rounds. Vasquez left the sport with a record of eighty-two fights (winning sixty-eight, losing thirteen, and drawing one). Vasquez also has the distinction of making more defences in any one year of the WBA world super-welterweight title than any other fighter at the weight at that time. The event took place in 1994 when he successfully defended the title on six occasions.

Amir Khan lived up to the high expectations fight pundits had of him on 18 July 2009 when he put on a skilled ring performance to win the WBA super-lightweight title over twelve rounds. Khan took the crown from defending Ukraine champion Andriy Kotelink. The contest took place at the M.E.N. Arena in Manchester.

When Joe Calzaghe retired from boxing in 2009, he did so with an unblemished professional record of forty-six bouts, having won the

Above left: Don Broadhurst became the first holder of the Commonwealth super-flyweight title in 2008. (*Philip Sharkey*)

Above right: Amir Khan seen wearing his Commonwealth lightweight belt won the WBA world super-lightweight crown in 2009. (*Les Clark*)

WBO, IBF, WBC, and WBA versions of the world super-middleweight title during his time in the 'punch for pay' ranks. Joe also shared the record along with Germany's Sven Ottke of making the most defences of the championship at that time in the division a total of twenty-one. During his time in the ring, Calzaghe met a number of quality fighters who at had one time or another held a world title during their careers, these being Chris Eubank Jr (WBO middleweight and WBO super-middleweight), Robin Reid (WBC super-middleweight), Richie Woodhall (WBC super-middleweight), Charles Brewer (IBF super-middleweight), Byron Mitchell (WBA super-middleweight), Jeff Lacy, (IBF super-middleweight) Sakio Bika (WBC super midddlewight), Mikkel Kessler (WBA and WBC super-middleweight), Bernard Hopkins (undisputed middleweight and WBC and IBF light-heavyweight), and Roy Jones Jr (IBF middleweight, IBF

Joe Calzaghe retired from boxing with an undefeated professional record in 2009. (*Les Clark*)

super-middleweight, and WBC, WBA, and IBF light-heavyweight and WBA heavyweight).

David Haye packed his bags and travelled to Germany on 7 November 2009 to challenge Russian Nikolay Valuev for the WBA world heavyweight title. It was obvious when the fight was announced that this was not going to be an easy task for the challenger. The champion had a height advantage over Haye standing at 7 feet 2 inches—a problem the 6-foot 3-inch Englishman had to overcome. The event took place at the Arena Nurnberger in Versicherung, Nuremberg; it was not a thrill-a-minute encounter, not one to keep those in attendance on the edge of their seats. There had been more enthralling world title bouts in the division in the past—that was undeniable. However, Haye boxed intelligently and used his considerable boxing skills and clever tactics to outsmart the defending title-holder. At the end of twelve rounds, it was a case of mission accomplished when Haye's hand was lifted aloft in victory, seeing him crowned the new champion. Haye hence became the second former world cruiserweight king (WBA, WBC, and WBO) to win this title and the first British boxer to hold a version of the world heavyweight crown since Lennox Lewis.

David Haye defeated
Nikolay Valuev in 2009
to win the WBA world
heavyweight title.
(*Philip Sharkey*)

On 29 January 2010, Beibut Shumenov of Kazakhstan won the WBA world light-heavyweight title and the IBA crown when he outpointed defending champion Gabriel Campillo of Spain over twelve rounds at the Hard Rock Hotel and Casino in Las Vegas, Nevada. Shumenov gained revenge and a degree of satisfaction for a past defeat at the hands of Campillo, who had previously outpointed him over the twelve-round distance. This event took place when Campillo defended the crown against Shumenov on 15 August 2009 at the Sports Complex Daulet in Astana, Kazakhstan. In winning the championship on his second attempt, Shumenov created a record at the time by winning the title in just his tenth professional bouts. No previous boxer in the division had ever won a major version of this title with so few bouts behind him.

At York Hall in Bethnal Green, London, on 12 February 2010, London's Lenny Daws defended his British super-lightweight title against Welshman Jason Cook, a former European lightweight champion. The two fighters battled hard for the full twelve rounds, giving the fans a good night of boxing. Daws retained his championship. However, a clear winner could not be found and for the first time in a domestic title bout in this division, a draw was given by the ringside judges.

Alan Rudkin MBE passed away on 22 September 2010. Rudkin (aged sixty-eight years, nine months, and twenty-five days) was a class fighter who could be considered unlucky not to have won a world title during his career. In another era, it might have been a different story for Rudkin, who would have certainly attained the status of world champ. Yet when looking at Alan's career, he did not do too badly at all, having won the British bantamweight crown on two occasions, the Commonwealth title three times, and the European bantamweight championship. Alan fought a number of quality opponents men like Johnny Caldwell (world bantamweight champion European version, British flyweight, and British and Commonwealth bantamweight king), Fighting Harada (undisputed world bantamweight and flyweight champion), Lionel Rose (undisputed world bantamweight and Commonwealth holder), Ruben Olivares (undisputed world bantamweight and WBA and WBC featherweight title-holder), Walter McGowan (lineal world flyweight and British and Commonwealth title-holder and British and Commonwealth bantamweight champion) twice, Mimoun Ben Ali (European bantamweight) twice, Evan Armstrong (British featherweight champion), Franco Zurlo (European bantamweight champion), Johnny Clark (British and European bantamweight champion) twice, Jimmy Revie (British featherweight champion), Augustin Senin (European bantamweight champion), and Bob Allotey (European bantamweight champion). Rudkin closed his career with a fight record of fifty bouts (winning forty-two and losing eight).

On 23 October 2010, Kazakhstan-born and German resident Christina Hammer had the distinction of becoming the first holder of the women's WBO world middleweight title. Hammer won the vacant crown when she outpointed Bermuda-born Teresa Perozzi over ten rounds. The venue for the bout was the Erdgas Arena in Riesa, Germany. Perozzi recovered from this defeat and in her very next contest, which took place on 30 December 2011, she travelled to the Woodebrook Youth Centre in Port-of-Spain, Trinidad and Tobago, to confront Lorissa Rivas, also from the USA. The bout was for the first women's WBA version of the world middleweight title. On this outing, Perozzi triumphed when she won the crown with a ten-round points decision

Right: Alan Rudkin sadly passed away in 2010. (*Derek Rowe*)

Below: Johnny Clark (left) with Alan Rudkin. (*Derek Rowe*)

10

Round Ten: 2011–2017

On 7 May 2011, American Evander Holyfield (the first fighter to win a major version of the world heavyweight championship on four separate occasions and former world cruiserweight title-holder) said goodbye to boxing when he had his last contest, stopping Dane Brian Nielsen in round ten of a contest set for the duration of twelve in Koncerthuset, Copenhagen. During his time in the paid ranks, Holyfield took part in fifty-seven bouts (winning forty-four, losing ten, and drawing two with one no contest). He participated in six world cruiserweight contests and twenty world heavyweight championship bouts. In the professional ring, Holyfield fought the very best and amazingly met twenty-two fighters who at one time or another held a major version of the world crown; these men were Tyrone Booze (WBO cruiserweight), Dwight Muhammad Qawi (WBA cruiserweight), Ricky Parkey (IBF cruiserweight), Ossie Ocasio (WBA cruiserweight), Carlos De Leon (WBC cruiserweight), Pinklon Thomas (WBC heavyweight), Michael Dokes (WBA heavyweight), James Douglas (undisputed heavyweight), George Foreman (undisputed heavyweight), Larry Holmes (WBC and IBF heavyweight), Riddick Bowe (undisputed heavyweight), Michael Moorer (WBO light-heavyweight and WBO and IBF heavyweight), Ray Mercer (WBO heavyweight), Bobby Czyz (IBF light-heavyweight and WBA cruiserweight), Mike Tyson (undisputed heavyweight), Lennox Lewis (undisputed heavyweight), John Ruiz (WBA heavyweight), Hasim Rahman (WBC heavyweight), Chris Byrd (WBO and IBF heavyweight), James Toney (IBF middleweight, super-middleweight, and cruiserweight), Sultan Ibragimov (WBO heavyweight), and Nikolay Valuev (WBA heavyweight).

On 21 May 2011, former world middleweight title-holder Bernard Hopkins of America stepped into the ring at the Bell Centre in Montreal,

Canada, to challenge the reigning WBC light-heavyweight champion Jean Pascal for the crown. This was their second meeting since in a previous challenge for the championship on 18 December 2010, Hopkins failed to lift the title when Canadian Pascal held on to the crown by way of a draw over twelve rounds. Their first encounter had also taken place in Canada, the venue being the Pepsi Coliseum, Quebec. The return contest once again went the full duration of twelve rounds, when Hopkins this time claimed the championship when given the points decision. The American (at the age of forty-six years, four months, and six days) became at that time the oldest man to win a world title in the sport. The defeated champion Pascal was twenty-eight years, six months, and twenty-three days.

Julio Cesar Chavez Jr of Mexico won the WBC version of the world middleweight championship on 4 June 2011 when he outpointed holder Sebastian Zbik of Germany over twelve rounds at Staples Center in Los Angeles, California. In so doing, he emulated his father (Julio Cesar Chavez) to some degree by becoming a world title-holder. While Jr did well to claim a world championship, he had some way to go world title wise before he caught up to his father who was an outstanding fighter. Before he retired from the ring, Chavez Sr won the following world crowns: WBC super-featherweight, WBC and WBA lightweight, and WBC and IBF super-lightweight.

Colin Lynes boxed his way to a twelve round points decision on 9 November 2011 to capture the British welterweight crown from defending title-holder Lee Purdy. The contest between the two fighters, who both hailed from Essex, took place at York Hall in Bethnal Green, London. It was a special night for Lynes, who produced a fine display of boxing. A former British super-lightweight champion, Lynes moved up a weight division to win this championship. Lynes was also a former holder of both the IBO version of the world super-lightweight title and was a former holder of the European championship at the weight. Going into the bout, Purdy was considered by some to be the favourite to retain the title, but Lynes showed that he still had a great deal left and proved the doubters wrong.

Two sons of former world champions locked horns at the Arena Jorge Cuesy Serrano in Tuxtla Gutiérrez, Mexico, on 17 December 2011. The two Mexican fighters who squared up to each other were Jorge Paez Jr and Omar Chavez. Paez Jr (the son of Jorge Paez, the former WBO and IBF world featherweight king) entered the fray with a record of thirty-five fights (winning twenty-nine, losing four, with one draw, and one no contest). Omar Chavez (the younger son of Julio Cesar Chavez, the former WBC super-featherweight, WBA and WBC lightweight, and WBC and IBF super-lightweight) had a slate comprising of twenty-eight fights (winning

Colin Lynes won a second British title in 2011. (*Philip Sharkey*)

twenty-seven with one draw). When considering their past performances, Chavez looked to have the edge in this meeting. The contest went the full ten rounds and saw Chavez defeated for the first time with Paez Jr earning a ten-round points decision in a lively contest.

On 23 March 2012, at the Civic Hall, Wolverhampton, former WBO world and European cruiserweight champion Enzo Maccarinelli walked into the ring to battle for the British crown in the weight division. The title-holder was Shane McPhilbin, who was making the first defence of the championship. Prior to the fight, you would have to tip Maccarinelli to win since he had the most experience, having taken part in thirty-nine contests (winning thirty-four and losing five) against a number of top-flight fighters. By contrast, McPhilbin had only participated in ten bouts (winning eight and losing two); he had not mixed with the same level of opposition as his challenger had. The two fighters put on an entertaining night for the paying punters, letting their punches go freely. In a bizarre first round, Maccarinelli was put down and looked almost out. McPhilbin looked to be on the verge of a big upset and the best victory of his boxing life. Maccarinelli bravely beat the count and rose to his feet; he looked hurt and ready for the taking. Then confusion ensued when the bell sounded, causing the stanza to come to a premature end with forty-seven seconds still left on the clock. The exciting fight continued with more drama when once again, Maccarinelli found himself on the canvas for a count in round three. In round nine, it was McPhilbin's turn to sit on the canvas for a count. It appeared when taking account of the hurtful punches thrown and then landing on both fighters that the contest would most certainly end inside the distance. However, the contest lasted the full twelve rounds, with Maccarinelli taking the title on points. On winning the championship, Maccarinelli became the first Welshman to hold a British title in this division.

At the women's world championship, which took place in Qinhuangdao, China, middleweight Savannah Marshall excelled when she became Britain's first female amateur world boxing champion; Marshall outpointed opponent Elena Vystropova of Azerbaijan 17–15 on 19 May 2012 to take the gold medal. While Marshall was a good solid exponent of boxing, her victory proved to be a surprise and a welcome boost for UK amateur boxing.

The London 2012 Olympic Games saw the introduction of female boxers, where Nicola Adams flyweight (UK), Katie Taylor lightweight (Ireland), and Claressa Shields (America) middleweight all won gold in their respective weight divisions. Nicole Adams captured the respective gold and made history by becoming the first woman to do so when she outpointed China's Ren Cancan over four rounds 16–7. Katie Taylor secured her gold medal and ensured her place at the top of the podium when she outpointed Russia's Sofya Ochigava 10–8. Claressa Shields won gold when she outpointed Russia's Nadezhda Torlopova 19–12.

A historical event took place at the Bodymaker Colosseum in Osaka, Japan on 20 June 2012 when WBC world minimumweight title-holder Kazuto Ioka met his rival in the shape of WBA world title champion Akira Yaegashi. This contest was the first world unification bout between two Japanese boxers. The two fighters gave it their all and at the end of the twelve-round contest, Ioka emerged the victor and hence unified champion when he outpointed his opponent.

A controversial contest took place on 14 July 2012 when David Haye and Dereck Chisora crossed gloves in an anticipated and well-documented grudge match at Upton Park in West Ham, London. Going into the contest, Haye was a former WBA, WBC, and WBO world cruiserweight king and former WBA world heavyweight champion. Both men threw punches with mean intentions from the very start of the ten-round contest; it was obvious that the bout would not last the scheduled route. David used his skills and hence fought his way to victory, stopping Chisora (the former

British and Commonwealth heavyweight title-holder) in round five in a bout licensed by the Luxembourg Boxing Federation and not the British Boxing Board of Control. The vacant WBO international heavyweight title and the vacant WBA intercontinental heavyweight crown were on the line during the contest.

England's Robin Reid stepped into the professional boxing ring at the Sheffield Arena in Yorkshire for the last time on 20 October 2012 to face Kenny Anderson of Scotland for the vacant British super-middleweight crown. It did not end well for Reid, who was stopped in round five of a contest set for twelve. Reid left the boxing scene with a record of fifty-one fights (winning forty-two, losing eight, and drawing one of his previous encounters). During his time in the 'punch for pay' code, Reid won many honours in the ring, which included the WBC world super-middleweight crown and other title belts at the weight, including the IBO and WBF championships. Reid also shared the ring with ten fighters who had had one time or another held a version of the world championship: Vincenzo Nardiello (WBC super-middleweight), Hacine Cherifi (WBC middleweight), Thulani Malinga (WBC super-middleweight), Joe Calzaghe (WBO, IBF, WBC, and WBA super-middleweight), Silvio Branco (WBA light-heavyweight), Julio Cesar Vasquez (WBA super-welterweight), Sven Ottke (IBF and WBA super-middleweight), Brian Magee (WBA super-middleweight), Jeff Lacy (IBF super-middleweight), and Carl Froch (WBC, IBF, and WBA super-middleweight). Reid also excelled in the amateur ranks, winning a bronze medal at light middleweight in the 1992 Olympic Games, which were held in Barcelona, Spain.

Chao Zhong Xiong had his name inserted into the record books when he became the first professional boxer from China to win a world title. He accomplished this feat on 24 November 2012, outpointing Mexico's Javier Martinez Resendiz over twelve rounds at the Kunming City Stadium in China to capture the vacant WBC minimum flyweight crown.

On 30 November 2012, Andrew 'Freddie' Flintoff found that he was not stumped or indeed caught out in his new sport when he made his professional boxing debut at heavyweight. Flintoff outpointed American Richard Dawson over four rounds at the Manchester Arena in Manchester, Lancashire. Flintoff was a former renowned cricketer who had played for Lancashire and England during his respected career.

Northern Ireland's Commonwealth super-bantamweight champion Carl Frampton was bad news for Spain's Kiko Martinez. On 9 February 2013, they met at the Odyssey Arena, Belfast in a contest that saw Marinez making the second defence of his European crown with Frampton's IBF intercontinental title also on the line. Frampton showed his class and retained his crown; he also emerged as the new EBU champion when

Above left: Dereck Chisora was involved in a controversial contest with David Haye in 2012. (*Les Clark*)

Above right: Former WBC world super-middleweight king Robin Reid had his last professional contest in 2012. (*Les Clark*)

he stopped his opponent in round nine of twelve. Martinez overcame this defeat and won the IBF world super-bantamweight championship on 17 August 2013. In his third defence of the world title, he again met Frampton on 6 September 2014, the venue being the Titanic Quarter in Belfast, Northern Ireland. However, this was not a chance for the Spaniard to gain revenge over Frampton as once again, Martinez suffered a defeat when he lost his world crown by a twelve-round points decision.

Puerto Rican-born Amanda Serrano faced opponent Wanda Pena Ozuna on 16 February 2013 at the Gran Arena del Cibao in Santiago de los Caballeros, the Dominican Republic. Two vacant championships were up for grabs: the WIBA and UBF female world featherweight titles. Fighting on home turf, Ozuna was keen to win the crowns but Serrano had other ideas, stopping her in the opening session of a ten-round contest. On this occasion, Serrano became the first to hold the UBF version of the title in the division. Serrano now had a record of nineteen fights (winning seventeen, losing one, and drawing one); Ozuna's résumé read thirteen fights (eight wins and five defeats).

On 23 February 2013, Ishe Smith outpointed fellow American defending champion Cornelius Bundrage over twelve rounds to capture the IBF world super-welterweight crown at the Masonic Temple in Detroit, Michigan. In so doing, Smith became the first Las Vegas-born fighter to win a world championship.

Bernard Hopkins certainly showed the young pups a thing or two and laughed in the face of Father Time on 9 March 2013 at the Barclays Centre in Brooklyn, New York. The American showed that he was not yet ready for the rocking chair by the fireside along with a pair of comfortable slippers. Hopkins outpointed countryman and defending IBF world light-heavyweight champion Tavoris Cloud over twelve rounds to capture the title. The former undisputed world middleweight king and WBC world light-heavyweight champion, Hopkins broke his previous record when he became the oldest man at that time in the sport's history to win a world championship at the age of forty-eight years, one month, and twenty-two days. Tavoris was aged thirty-one years, one month, and twenty-seven days and was undefeated in twenty-four previous bouts. Hopkins was showing that age really is just a number.

Christina McMahon contributed to the history of the sport when she became the first female boxer to top a fight card in Ireland on 9 March 2013. Christina did not disappoint those in attendance when she put in an excellent performance to outpoint opponent Karina Kopinska of Poland over eight rounds at the Fairways Hotel in Dundalk to take her undefeated record to five victories.

Puerto Rican Cindy Serrano made short work of her opponent Grecia Nova on 10 May 2013 when contesting the vacant UBF world female super-featherweight crown. The bout saw Nova (who was fighting in front of her home fans at the Coliseo de Boxeo Carlos Teo Cruz in Santo Domingo, Dominican Republic) stopped in the first round of a scheduled ten. The win by Serrano made a mark in the history books since for the first time, two sisters held a world crown at the same time (Serrano's younger sibling Amanda was the reigning IBA and UBF world featherweight title-holder).

On 11 May 2013, former British, European, and Commonwealth bantamweight champion Jamie McDonnell won the vacant IBF world championship at the Keepmoat Stadium in Doncaster by outpointing Mexico's Julio Ceja over twelve rounds. Going into the contest, McDonnell had won twenty bouts with two defeats and one draw. Ceja entered the ring with impressive credentials, having an unblemished record of twenty-four victories. The task for McDonnell was clearly not an easy one. As his record suggested, Ceja was an excellent, well-schooled boxer who would not submit to defeat without making a fight of it; he was not easy pickings and not a victim brought in to occupy the opposite corner. Mexico had produced many good, indeed great, world champions in the bantamweight division over the years and Ceja had every intention of adding his name to the illustrative list. Ceja, as expected, pushed McDonnell hard throughout the contest, looking to land the punches that would see him take the title home. The Briton was not able to relax for one minute during the intense twelve-round battle which took place inside the ring. However, McDonnell boxed extremely well to gain a deserved victory over his opponent. The win over Ceja gave McDonnell the distinction of being the first boxer from Doncaster to win a world championship.

On 25 July 2013, Kyotaro Fujimoto stopped Ugandan Okello Peter in round six of ten at the Korakuen Hall in Tokyo to win the vacant Japanese heavyweight title. The crown may have been covered in cobwebs and dust for this was the first Japanese championship contest in this weight division since 4 May 1957. On that occasion, Noburu Kataoka won the inaugural crown by outpointing Yutaka Nakagoshi over ten rounds at the Kyobashi Hall in Tokyo. Soon after Kataoka won the title, the division was abolished due to the lack of boxers at the weight.

While one brother in a fighting family winning a world title is an achievement, and two is something to sit up and take notice of, three is something very special. Such an occasion took place on 1 August 2013 when Tomoki Kameda of Japan outpointed defending champion Paulus Ambunda of Namibia over twelve rounds at the Cebu City Waterfront Hotel and Casino Barangay in Lahug, the Philippines, to capture the WBO world bantamweight championship. Tomoki's brother Koki was, at the time, the reigning WBA world bantamweight title-holder while the other sibling, Daiki, was a former WBA world flyweight king.

Liam Smith won the vacant British super-welterweight crown on 21 September 2013 when he outpointed Erick Ochieng over twelve rounds at the Olympia in Liverpool. In so doing, he made history on the night as he joined brothers Paul (super-middleweight) and Stephen (super-featherweight) as reigning British title-holders. This was the first time that three siblings had held a British championship simultaneously.

One had to ask on 26 October 2013 whether there was no stopping this man when American Bernard Hopkins continued to prove that age was no barrier when it came to world title bouts. He made a successful defence of his IBF world light-heavyweight crown against challenger Karo Murat (who was born in Armenia but lived in Germany) at the Broadwalk Hall in Atlantic City, New Jersey. In retaining his crown on points over twelve rounds, Bernard, who was no stranger when it came to creating records in the sport, became (at the age of forty-eight years, nine months, and eleven

Bernard Hopkins continues
to prove age is no barrier in
a boxing ring.
(*Philip Sharkey*)

days) the oldest man at that time to successfully defend a major world
title. Murat was thirty years, one month, and twenty-four days old.

The Davis family had very little luck when boxing in the UK. On 16
November 2013, Dyah Davis challenged England's James DeGale for the
WBC silver super-middleweight title at the Glow in Bluewater, Kent. The
American failed in his attempt to win the championship when Degale
outpointed him over twelve rounds. Going back in time to 7 June 1980 at
Ibrox Park in Glasgow, Scotland, Dyah's father (Howard Davis Jr) made
the trip to Britain to challenge Jim Watt for the WBC world lightweight
crown. The challenger was undefeated in thirteen professional bouts and
based on his record appeared at first sight to be on the inexperienced side.
It certainly did not stack up well against Watt's slate of forty-three bouts
with seven defeats. However, Davis Jr was a sound technical boxer who
many followers of the sport felt was a king in waiting. Davis Jr was a
smooth operator who had an impressive amateur pedigree, having been
an Olympic gold medallist at lightweight in 1976; he also collected the
Val Barker award for being the outstanding boxer of the games. On the
night, Watt more than proved his worth as champion when he outboxed
his opponent over fifteen rounds to retain his title.

On 8 March 2014, Josh Goodwin promoted a show at York Hall in Bethnal Green, London. At that moment in time, Josh became the youngest promoter in boxing at the age of eighteen years, five months, and seventeen days.

Japan's Naoya Inoue clearly believed in the old saying 'time waits for no man' when he won the WBC light-flyweight world title on 6 April 2014 stopping defending champion Adrian Hernandez of Mexico in the sixth round of twelve; the venue was the Ota-City General Gymnasium in Tokyo. At the age of twenty years, eleven months, and twenty-seven days, Inoue became a champion in fast time since this was just his sixth professional contest.

Bernard Hopkins, still pushing the boundaries, gave heart to all those over forty who felt they were past it and that their better days were behind them. If the American was slowing down, it did not show since Hopkins created yet another boxing record on 19 April 2014. Hopkins (the IBF world light-heavyweight champion) became, at the age of forty-nine years, three months, and four days, the oldest boxer to not only defend a world crown but also to unify one when he outpointed WBA world light-heavyweight and IBA title-holder Beibut Shumenov (born in Kazakhstan but resident in the USA) over twelve rounds at the DC Armory in Washington, Columbia. Shumenov was aged thirty years and eight months (the IBA version of the title was not on the line during this contest).

Australian Sam Soliman pulled off a surprise when he won the IBF version of the world middleweight crown on 31 May 2014, outpointing holder Felix Sturm of Germany over twelve rounds. The battle for the crown took place at the König Palast in Krefeld, Germany. By winning, Soliman became, at the age of forty years, six months, and eighteen days, the oldest man to capture a version of the championship in this division.

It was a grudge match and the most anticipated return contest between two fighters in a prize ring in the UK for a number of years. The contest pitted IBF and WBA super-middleweight champion Carl Froch, defending his laurels, against challenger and fellow Briton George Groves at Wembley Stadium, London, on 31 May 2014. A reported 80,000 fans watched the exciting action take place, where Froch, in a thrilling encounter, retained his titles with a stunning stoppage in round eight in a contest scheduled for twelve. In their previous contest on 23 November 2013 at the Phones 4u Arena in Manchester, Froch had halted Groves in round nine of twelve after being heavily floored in the first round by his hard-punching challenger. The stoppage by Froch at that time was controversial since many pundits considered the stoppage a little premature, which set the wheels in motion for a return contest where the champion put any arguments about his first victory to rest with his display.

Carl Froch was put on the deck in the first round by challenger George Groves in their first meeting during 2013. (*Philip Sharkey*)

At the StubHub Center in Carson, California, Vasyl Lomachenko of Ukraine put in a fine performance to confirm his potential and hence justified the high expectations many pundits had of him when he outpointed American opponent Gary Russell Jr over twelve rounds on 21 June 2014 to capture the vacant WBO world featherweight title in just his third professional bout. This feat, which can only be called outstanding, saw him equal the record of former WBC super-lightweight champion Saensak Muangsurin of Thailand, winning a world crown with the fewest contests.

Michaela Walsh (Northern Ireland) outpointed Thessa Dumas (Mauritius) over four two-minute rounds in a flyweight contest at the Commonwealth Games on 28 July 2014 in the first-ever women's boxing contest to take place at this event.

Flyweight Nicola Adams won on points over four two-minute rounds (a split decision) against Michaela Walsh on 2 August 2014 at the Commonwealth Games to become the first female to capture a boxing gold medal at this event.

American Anthony Dirrell won the WBC world super-middleweight title when he outpointed holder Cameroon-born and Australian resident Sakio Bika over twelve rounds at the StubHub Center on 16 August

2014. In a previous challenge for this crown, Dirrell was awarded a twelve-round draw against Bika on 7 December 2013 at the Barclays Center in Brooklyn, New York. In winning this championship, Anthony had succeeded where his older brother failed, since on 17 October 2009, Andre Dirrell challenged the then WBC king Carl Froch of the UK at the Nottingham Arena, England but failed to take the crown when outpointed over twelve rounds.

Serbia-born German Marco Huck successfully defended his WBO world cruiserweight title on 30 August 2014 against Italy's Mirko Larghetti by way of a twelve-round points decision at the Gerry Weber Stadium in Halle, Germany. This was a special night for Huck in more ways than one since on the night he equalled England's Johnny Nelson's record of making the most title defences in the division, which stood at thirteen.

In a unification fight on 13 September 2014, Norway-based Columbian Cecilia Braekhus (the WBC, WBA, and WBO world welterweight champion) met Croatian Ivana Habazin (the IBF holder) at the Tap 1 in Copenhagen, Denmark. At the end of the ten-round contest, Braekhus emerged the victor by taking a points decision and in so doing became the first women to become an undisputed world champion.

England's Anthony Joshua (the former 2012 Olympic gold medal winner at super heavyweight) showed promise in winning his first professional title on 11 October 2014 by stopping Russia's Denis Bakhtov for the vacant WBC international heavyweight crown in the second round of ten at the 02 Arena (Millenium Dome) in Greenwich, London.

On 25 October 2014, reigning British and Commonwealth flyweight champion Kevin Satchell won the European crown at the Echo Arena in Liverpool, outpointing Belarus-born Spaniard Valery Yanchy over twelve rounds. It is amazing to note that Satchell was the first UK boxer to hold the European title in this division since Northern Ireland's Damaen Kelly, who both won and relinquished the crown in 2000.

On 8 November 2014, Russian Sergey Kovalev (the WBO world light-heavyweight king) met the reigning IBF and WBA king Bernard Hopkins of America at the Broadwalk Hall in Atlantic City in a unification contest. At the end of the twelve-round bout, Kovalev emerged the victor with a points decision. While Hopkins may have lost the fight, he created a record of being the oldest man at the age of forty-nine years, nine months, and twenty-four days to defend a world title.

Greek-born but an American resident Sonya Lamonakis outpointed American Carlette Ewell over ten rounds on 6 December 2014 at the LB Scott Sports Auditorium in Phillipsburg, Sint Maarten to win the vacant IBO women's world heavyweight title. Sonya has the distinction of being the first woman in this division to hold this particular version of the crown.

Former WBA world heavyweight champion Ernie Terrell, who was born on 4 April 1939, passed away on 16 December 2014. During his career, Terrell comprised a record of fifty-five fights (winning forty-six and losing nine). Ernie fought a host of top-flight boxers, including Muhammad Ali, Cleveland Williams (twice), Zora Folley, Bob Foster, Eddie Machen, George Chuvalo, Doug Jones, and Thad Spencer.

Japan's Naoya Inoue punched his way to a world title in a second weight division on 30 December 2014 at the Metropolitan Gym in Tokyo. Having already won the WBC light-flyweight championship, Inoue knocked out holder Omar Andres Narvaez of Argentina in two rounds of twelve to capture the WBO super-flyweight title. It was amazing to note that this was only Inoue's eighth professional contest.

One of the many great songs that The Beatles wrote and sang during their career was 'Back in the U.S.S.R.'. However, on 17 January 2015, it was a clear case of back in the USA when Deontay Wilder became the first American to hold a version of the world heavyweight title since Shannon Briggs, who held the WBO crown from 2006 to 2007. There must have been a big sigh of relief from American fight fans when Wilder accomplished this feat by outpointing holder Haitian-born Canadian Bermane Stiverne over twelve rounds at the MGM Grand in Las Vegas, Nevada.

It was the fight everyone had wanted to see a contest between two fighters considered to be the very best in their weight division with very little between them talent wise. However, many pundits feared that it would never happen. Then the bout was signed and sealed, thus the meeting of American Floyd Mayweather Jr and Manny Pacquiao of the Philippines was on. The bout, which duly took place at the MGM Grand in Las Vegas on 2 May 2015, gathered a great deal of media attention; this was expected for such a giant sporting event between two fighters considered to be among the greats of their era and thus fated to be included in the International Hall of Fame when their careers came to an end. The two boxers put their respective world welterweight titles on the line in a unification contest. Mayweather Jr was defending his WBC welterweight and WBA super world welterweight crown while Pacquiao was putting the WBO version of the championship on the line. Floyd entered the ring with an undefeated record of forty-seven bouts pitted against his rival's résumé of sixty-four fights with fifty-seven wins, five losses, and two draws. At the end of the twelve-round encounter, Mayweather Jr emerged the victor on points.

It looked as if Jamie McDonnell (a former British, Commonwealth, European, and IBF world bantamweight king) would meet with defeat on 9 May 2015. McDonnell travelled to Texas to defend his WBA world

Floyd Mayweather Jr defeated
his rival Manny Pacquiao in
2015. (*Les Clark*)

bantamweight crown against the former WBO world bantamweight king Tomoki Kameda of Japan, who was undefeated in thirty-one bouts. McDonnell had a slate of twenty-five wins, two defeats, and one draw. The venue was the State Farm Arena, Hidalgo. Kameda revealed the skills that had previously taken him to a world title when he floored McDonnell for a count in the third round; it could be said that the outcome for McDonnell did not look too good. However, the British fighter showed his fighting heart to overcome this setback at the early stage of the contest. The Briton hence dug down and outpointed his challenger over twelve rounds to retain his championship.

James Degale, the former British and European super-middleweight title-holder, fought his way into the boxing history books when he ventured to the Agganis Arena in Boston, Massachusetts, on 23 May 2015. Degale had to confront American Andre Dirrell for the vacant IBF world super-middleweight championship, which fellow Briton Carl Froch had previously relinquished. Dirrell was a tough fighter for Degale to overcome, especially so when considering that he was to swap punches with him in his own country. Degale was up for the challenge; this was his moment to make a statement and make a statement he did. Degale put on a fine performance to ensure that the title stayed in Britain. The contest went the full distance of twelve rounds between the two southpaws and when the final bell rang to conclude the contest, Degale emerged the victor on points. In so doing, he became the first British Olympic gold medal winner to capture a professional world title. Degale had won the gold at middleweight in the 2008 Olympic Games, which had taken place in Beijing, China. British-born Lennox Lewis won a gold medal at super heavyweight at the 1988 Seoul Olympics and went on to capture the world heavyweight championship, but he was representing Canada on the occasion he won that medal.

On 30 May 2015, Kell Brook made a successful second defence of his IBF world welterweight crown at the O2 Arena (Millenium Dome) when he stopped challenger Frankie Gavin in round six of a scheduled twelve to retain his crown. Gavin was a good fighter but was unable to cope with what Brook bought to the ring. Brook was clearly a league above his challenger—a fact that revealed itself very early in the contest. This was the first time that two Britons had fought each other in a contest for a major version of the world welterweight crown.

Nicola Adams made history once again when she became the first woman to win a boxing gold medal at the European Games held in Baku, Azerbaijan. To accomplish this feat, Nicola outpointed Poland's Sandra Drabik over three rounds in the final, which took place on 25 June 2015.

It looked as if it was all going to go horribly wrong when defending IBF world super-bantamweight champion Carl Frampton made his USA debut on 18 July 2015 against Mexican challenger Alejandro Gonzalez Jr at the Don Haskins Convention Center in El Paso, Texas. It appeared that a confident-looking Gonzalez Jr was on his way to victory and was thus going to emulate his father and win a world title when he floored Fampton twice in the first round. However, the defending champion refused to submit and fought his way back after the shaky start and won a twelve-round points decision. Gonzalez Jr was the son of namesake Alejandro Gonzalez Sr, a former holder of the WBC world featherweight title.

Kelly Morgan made her professional boxing debut on 18 July 2015, stopping Klaudia Vigh of Hungary in one round of a scheduled six. The contest took place at the Bath Pavillion in Avon. When it came to sport, it appeared that Kelly was something of an all-rounder since she had won a bronze medal for the javelin event at the 2002 Manchester Commonwealth Games.

Claressa Shields, the former 2012 Olympic Games gold medal winner, looked like becoming one of the greats in women's amateur boxing when she duly fought her way into the history books. At the Pan American Games, which took place in Toronto, Canada, on 24 July 2015, Shields

James Degale became the first British Olympic gold medal winner to capture a professional world championship in 2015 (see below). (*Philip Sharkey*)

Left to right: three UK gold medal winners: Dick McTaggart (lightweight, 1956), James DeGale (middleweight, 2008), and Terry Spinks (flyweight, 1956). (*Philip Sharkey*).

Above left: Kell Brook proved too much for challenger Frankie Gavin in their 2015 IBF world welterweight title contest. (*Philip Sharkey*)

Above right: Frankie Gavin. (*Philip Sharkey*)

outpointed opponent Yenebier Guillen of the Dominican Republic over three rounds at the middleweight poundage to become the first American woman to win gold at this event.

Floyd Mayweather Jr successfully defended his WBC world welterweight and WBA super-welterweight titles against fellow American Andre Berto at the MGM Grand Arena in Las Vegas on 12 September 2015. Mayweather Jr had relinquished the WBO version of the championship. As expected, Floyd had too much skill for his opponent and smoothly outpointed him over twelve rounds and in the process equalled Rocky Marciano's undefeated record of forty-nine fights.

Someone's undefeated record had to go on 12 September 2015 when England's Anthony Joshua stepped into the ring at the 02 Arena (Millenium Dome) in Greenwich, London, to defend his WBC international crown and contest the vacant Commonwealth heavyweight title against Scotland's Gary Cornish. Joshua had an unblemished slate of thirteen victories all inside the scheduled distance with Cornish entering the fray with a perfect record of twenty-one wins, twelve ending before the final bell. Cornish met with his first professional defeat when Joshua stopped him in the opening round of twelve. Joshua thus became the first Olympic gold medal winner to hold the Commonwealth heavyweight title since Lennox Lewis, who reigned from 1992 to 1993.

On 16 October 2015, Kohei Kono successfully defended his WBA world super-flyweight title against challenger Koki Kameda at the UIC Pavillion in Chicago, Illinois, with a twelve-round points decision. This was a unique occasion since this was the first world championship to be staged in America between two rival Japanese boxers.

Boxing history was made on 7 November 2015 when Callum Smith showed his punching power when winning the vacant British super-middleweight title and by also defending his WBC silver super-middleweight crown in the opening round of a scheduled twelve. Callum hence became the fourth brother from the Smith family to have held a British title with siblings Stephen having won the feather and super-featherweight, Liam super-welterweight, and Paul super-middleweight. Smith easily stopped his opponent Rocky Fielding at the Echo Arena in Liverpool when he zeroed in to land his damaging blows.

Britain's Lee Haskins attained the status of IBF world bantamweight champion without throwing a punch. This situation occurred when Haskins ventured to the USA to challenge American holder Randy Caballero for the respective title. The bout was to take place on 21 November 2015 at the Mandalay Bay Hotel and Casino Events Centre in Las Vegas. However, Caballero failed to make the weight and the title was stripped from him and awarded to Haskins. Before being upgraded to full champion, Haskins had previously won the interim IBF world crown on 13 June 2015 at the Whitchurch Sports Centre in Bristol, stopping Japan's Ryosuke Iwasa in round six of a contest scheduled for twelve.

England's Tyson Fury provided a massive shock to the non-believers and proved that he could deliver the goods when, against all odds, he paid a visit to Germany on 28 November 2015. Fury entered the lion's den to challenge Wladimir Klitschko for the WBA, IBF, WBO, and IBO versions of the world heavyweight title. The brutal truth prior to Fury's challenge for the championship was that few, if any, expected him to bring the crown back to the UK. There were even some who felt that the champion would stop Fury before the final bell had sounded to bring the contest to a close. It was felt Klitschko would know too much for his challenger. However, after twelve rounds of boxing at the Esprit Area in Düsseldorf, Fury proved the doubters wrong when he became the new champion after securing a points decision. Klitschko may have lost his titles, but he

Left: Anthony Joshua extended his undefeated professional run when he won the vacant Commonwealth heavyweight title, stopping Gary Cornish in the first round in 2015. (*Philip Sharkey*)

Below: Anthony Joshua (left) proved too strong for Gary Cornish. (*Philip Sharkey*)

created a record at that time by taking part in more world heavyweight title bouts than any previous fighter, the total being twenty-eight. It was not all plain sailing for the new champion; sometimes, the hardest fights take place outside of the ring since days later, the IBF stripped Tyson of their version of the title since the Briton agreed to meet Klitschko in a return bout rather than their mandatory contender Vyacheslav Glazkov of Ukraine—such is boxing politics.

When Tyson Fury won the WBA, IBF, WBO, and IBO world heavyweight titles, he became at the reported height of 6 feet 9 inches, the second tallest man to win the world heavyweight crown. The tallest man was former WBA king Nikolay Valuev of Russia, who measured an incredible 7 feet 2 inches. When Tyson Fury defeated Wladimir Klitschko, he thus became the first white British world heavyweight champion since Bob Fitzsimmons, who reigned from 1897 to 1899.

It was a matter of bombs away when two hard-punching undefeated heavyweights met at the 02 Arena (Millenium Dome) on 12 December 2015. Anthony Joshua, with a perfect résumé of winning all of his fourteen

Tyson Fury shocked the pundits when he won the WBA, IBF, WBO, and IBO versions of the world heavyweight title in 2015.
(*Philip Sharkey*)

fights inside the scheduled distance, stepped into the ring to defend his Commonwealth and WBC international heavyweight titles. Also at stake was the vacant British crown. In the opposite corner was Dillian Whyte with a slate of sixteen bouts to his credit, thirteen victories coming by way of a stoppage or knockout. Both fighters had firepower in their mitts and could do some serious damage should their explosive punching land. It was an obvious conclusion that this fight would not go the full distance of twelve rounds. Someone had to lose for the first time in their professional careers and after an exciting slugfest, the man to taste defeat was Whyte, who was duly stopped in round seven.

Former WBO world cruiserweight champion Enzo Maccarinelli from Wales ventured to the VTB Arena in Moscow on 12 December 2015 to engage in a ten-round contest against Roy Jones Jr. The American was a former world champion in four weight divisions, these being IBF middleweight, IBF super-middleweight, undisputed light-heavyweight, and WBA heavyweight. The bout ended in round four by a knockout in favour of Maccarinelli The Welshman pulled off a good victory and the name of Jones Jr on his record looked good. Yet it was evident that the American was not the fighter of old, not the man who once amazed fans with his all-round skills. The decline in the American's ability was of course no fault of Maccarinelli, who could only fight whoever was put in front of him. Russia had proven a successful fighting venue for the Welshman since this was his second victory in the country. Previously, Maccarinelli had captured the vacant European cruiserweight title on 27 April 2010 when at the Yubileiny Sports Palace in Saint Petersburg; Maccarinelli wasted no time in stopping home fighter Alexander Kotlobay in the opening round of twelve.

On 19 December 2015, Billy Joe Saunders outpointed defending champion Andy Lee of Ireland over twelve rounds to capture the WBO world middleweight title at the Manchester Arena. At that moment in time, UK boxing was booming and could boast an all-time best record of having a total of twelve fighters who held a version of a world championship: Lee Haskins (IBF bantamweight), Jamie McDonnell (WBA regular bantamweight), Carl Frampton (IBF super-bantamweight), Scott Quigg (WBA regular super-bantamweight), Lee Selby (IBF featherweight), Terry Flanagan (WBO lightweight), Anthony Crolla (WBA lightweight), Kell Brook (IBF welterweight), Liam Smith (WBO super-welterweight), Billy Joe Saunders (WBO middleweight), James DeGale (IBF super-middleweight), and Tyson Fury (WBO WBA and IBO heavyweight).

On 16 January 2016, American Charles Martin won the vacant IBF world heavyweight crown when he stopped opponent Vyacheslav Glazkov of Ukraine in the third round of twelve at the Barclays Centre in Brooklyn, New York. In victory, Martin became just the sixth boxer with the southpaw stance to hold a major version of the championship in the heavyweight division since the introduction of the Queensberry rules. The previous five to box in that stance were Michael Moorer (USA), Chris Byrd (USA), Corrie Sanders (South Africa), Ruslan Chagaev (Uzbekistan), and Sultan Ibragimov (Russia).

Walter McGowan MBE passed away on 15 February 2016 aged seventy-three years, four months, and two days. Scotland's McGowan was an exceptionally gifted boxer who had forty professional bouts (winning thirty-two, losing seven, and drawing one). In the amateur ranks, Walter won the ABA flyweight title in 1961. In the 'punch for pay' code, McGowan won the linear world flyweight crown, plus the British and Commonwealth flyweight titles coupled with the British and Commonwealth bantamweight crowns. The Scott exchanged punches with class operatives like Salvatore Burruni (undisputed world flyweight champion) twice, Chartchai Chionoi (WBC and WBA world flyweight king) twice, Alan Rudkin twice, Tommaso Galli, Rene Libeer, Jose Medel, and Jackie Brown twice.

On 2 April 2016, British super-middleweight champion Callum Smith stepped into the ring at the Echo Arena, Liverpool to challenge reigning

Gary Jacobs (left) with former linear world flyweight champion Walter McGowan, who passed away in 2016. (*Derek Rowe*)

European title-holder Hadillah Mohoumadi of France. Smith gave his supporters plenty to cheer about when he won the crown in the first round by way of a stoppage in a bout scheduled for twelve. This was the first European title bout in the division to end in the opening stanza since 3 April 1992. On that occasion, it once again involved a British and a French fighter contesting the crown. The defending champion James Cook from the UK stepped between the ropes at the Vitrolles in Bouches-du-Rhône, France, and lost the title when knocked in the first round of twelve by home fighter Frank Nicotra.

On 9 April 2016, Gilberto Ramirez entered the ring at the MGM Grand Garden Arena in Las Vegas to challenge reigning WBO world super-middleweight title-holder Arthur Abraham. At the end of the twelve-round encounter, Ramirez became the first Mexican-born fighter to win a version of the world crown in this division. Ramirez dethroned the experienced German-based Armenian by way of a twelve-round points decision. Going into the bout, Ramirez had an impressive record, being undefeated in thirty-three professional bouts with Abraham comprising a record of forty-four victories with four defeats.

Anthony Joshua of Great Britain confirmed once again that he had concussive power in his mitts when he won the IBF world heavyweight championship. Joshua won the crown with ultimate ease, knocking out defending title-holder Charles Martin in round two on 9 April 2016 at the O2 Arena (Millenium Dome). Even before the bout got underway, few felt that the contest would go the full twelve rounds. At that moment, the UK had two reigning undefeated world champions in the weight division. Tyson Fury (the WBA, WBO, and IBO holder) had an unblemished record of twenty-five professional bouts with Joshua's record now standing at a perfect sixteen. It was happy days for the British heavyweight boxing scene. The WBC belt was owned by American Deontay Wilder, who was also undefeated in thirty-six fights at the time.

When Anthony Joshua defeated Charles Martin to become IBF heavyweight champion, he became just the second fighter to win a version of the title while still being the reigning Olympic champion. Joe Frazier was the first; he accomplished this feat when he stopped fellow American Buster Mathis on 4 March 1968 at Madison Square Garden in New York in round eleven of fifteen to capture the vacant NYSAC version of the world heavyweight crown. Frazier had won gold at heavyweight in the 1964 Olympic Games, which were held in Tokyo, Japan in 1964.

Anthony Joshua became the eleventh Olympic gold medallist to win a version of the world heavyweight championship when he defeated Charles Martin. Joshua won the medal at the 2012 London Games. Previous medal winners included Floyd Patterson (middleweight, 1952); Cassius

Above: Charles Martin (left) lost his IBF world heavyweight crown to Anthony Joshua in 2016. (*Philip Sharkey*)

Below: Joe Frazier won a version of the world heavyweight crown in 1968 while still the reigning Olympic champion (Frazier won gold at heavyweight in 1964 in Mexico). (*Derek Rowe*)

Clay (later M. Ali; light-heavyweight, 1960); Joe Frazier (heavyweight, 1964); George Foreman (heavyweight, 1968); Leon Spinks (light-heavyweight, 1976); Michael Spinks (middleweight, 1976); Ray Mercer (heavyweight, 1988); Lennox Lewis (super heavyweight, 1988); Wladimir Klitschko (super heavyweight, 1996); and Alexander Povetkin (super heavyweight, 2004).

On 16 April 2016, the first bout for a major world title was staged in New Zealand at The Trust Arena in Auckland. The two boxers from the USA—Kali Reis and Maricela Cornejo—duly entered the ring to confront each other for the vacant female WBC world middleweight crown. The contest went the full ten rounds and at the final bell, Reis was given the points decision and the championship belt.

Ryan Walsh, in defence of his British featherweight title on 30 April 2016, stopped challenger James Tennyson in the fifth round of twelve. At the same venue, which was the Copper Box Arena, Queen Elizabeth Olympic Park, London, Liam Walsh made a successful defence of his British super-featherweight crown in another scheduled twelve rounder that did not run its course. Liam stopped his challenger, Troy James, in the eighth round. This was the first time that twins had defended their respective British titles on the same fight card.

On 14 May 2016, Andrew Selby (younger brother of reigning IBF world featherweight champion Lee Selby) showed a great deal of promise when he won the vacant British flyweight title. The venue of the contest was the Ice Arena in Cardiff, Wales. Selby outpointed opponent Louis Norman over twelve rounds to take the respective crown. Selby achieved the distinction on this occasion of winning a British title faster than any previous Welsh fighter had to date. Selby won the crown in just his fifth professional bout. At this stage, it looked as if Selby would go on to higher honours in the boxing ring.

Ricky Burns won the vacant WBA world super-lightweight title on 28 May 2016 when he stopped Italian opponent Michele Di Rocco in round eight of twelve at the SSE Hydro in Glasgow, Scotland. Burns was making a habit of winning world championships. In this latest victory over Di Rocco, he became the first Scottish fighter to win a world crown in three different weight divisions and the third British-born exponent of boxing to achieve such a feat. Burns formerly held the world WBO super-featherweight title, winning this crown on 4 September 2010 by outpointing holder Roman Martinez of Puerto Rico over twelve rounds at the Kelvin Hall in Glasgow. Burns then added the WBO lightweight belt to his collection when he outpointed Australian Michael Katsidis over twelve rounds at Wembley Arena in London on 5 November 2011, winning the interim title. The Scot was later elevated to full champion and, on 10

March 2012 at the Braehead Arena in Glasgow, he made a first defence of the title, outpointing Paulus Moses of Namibia over twelve rounds. England's Bob Fitzsimmons (middleweight, heavyweight, and light-heavyweight) and Duke McKenzie (IBF flyweight WBO bantamweight and super-bantamweight) were the previous two fighters from the UK to hold triple world championships.

One of the true greats of heavyweight boxing, Muhammad Ali, sadly passed away on 3 June 2016 at the age of seventy-four years, four months, and seventeen days. Ali was born on 17 January 1942 in Louisville, Kentucky. Then known as Cassius Clay, he won the Olympic gold medal at light-heavyweight by outpointing Poland's Zbigniew Pietrzykowski at the 1960 Games, which took place in Rome, Italy. When turning professional, he eventually won the world heavyweight championship of the world, defeating the fearsome Sonny Liston who retired in the sixth round of fifteen. Ali was taking part in his twentieth contest in what was then considered at the time to be a massive upset. During his paid career, Ali participated in sixty-one bouts (winning fifty-six and losing five), twenty-five of which were for a world title. Ali crossed gloves with many top fighters during his paid career, ducking no one. Twelve of the fighters he met had at one time or another held a world championship. The respective fighters were Archie Moore (undisputed light-heavyweight), Sonny Liston (undisputed heavyweight) twice, Floyd Patterson (undisputed heavyweight) twice, Ernie Terrell (WBA heavyweight), Joe Frazier (undisputed heavyweight) three times, Jimmy Ellis (WBA heavyweight), Bob Foster (undisputed light-heavyweight), Ken Norton (WBC heavyweight) three times, George Foreman (undisputed heavyweight), Leon Spinks (undisputed heavyweight) twice, Larry Holmes (WBC and IBF heavyweight), and Trevor Berbick (WBC heavyweight). Ali became the first man to regain the heavyweight crown twice. Ali's name will always be remembered in the sporting world; of that, there is no doubt.

On 10 June 2016, England's Kelly Morgan won the vacant WBC silver middleweight crown when she outpointed Germany's Lisa Cielas over eight rounds at the Grange Leisure Centre in Swindon, Wiltshire. Thus Kelly became the first woman to hold this particular championship.

It was a proud day for Montenegro when the country saw its first-ever world boxing champion crowned on 11 June 2016. Dejan Zlaticanin stopped Bolivia's Franklin Mamani in round three of twelve to capture the vacant WBC lightweight title. The contest took place at the Turning Stone Resort and Casino in Verona, New York.

Ian Lewison jetted out to China to exchange blows in a professional manner with home fighter Zhiyu Wu on 24 June 2016 at the Guangxi Sports Center Gymnasium in Nanning. At stake was the vacant WBO Asia

Pacific heavyweight title. A win for Wu looked the likely outcome to the contest but Lewison had not come to lose and landed the finishing blow in round two of ten to grab the crown and become the first Briton to win this championship.

It was a contest that many fans were looking forward to: the challenge of former IBF and WBA world super-bantamweight champion Carl Frampton against the reigning super WBA world featherweight king Leo Santa Cruz of Mexico. Santa Cruz entered the ring at the Barclays Center in Brooklyn, New York, on 30 July 2016 with an undefeated record of thirty-three winning bouts with one draw and was a former IBF world bantamweight and WBC world super-bantamweight king. Frampton too entered the fray with an undefeated slate of twenty-two winning bouts. There were mixed views to some extent on who would emerge the victor in the contest. Experience was clearly with the defending champion, who had carved out a fine ring reputation. However, after twelve rounds of exciting action, Frampton took a points decision to become the new super WBA world featherweight king and produced a little ring history by becoming the first boxer from Northern Ireland to win a world crown in two different weight divisions. In winning the WBA world featherweight crown, Frampton emulated his manager Barry McGuigan, who held the crown from 1985 to 1986.

Nicola Adams successfully defended her gold medal in the flyweight division at the 2016 Olympic Games, which took place in Rio de Janeiro, Brazil, outpointing opponent Sarah Ourahmoune of France. Adams thus became the first British fighter since Harry Mallin to retain an Olympic title and hence win a second gold medal. Mallin had won gold at middleweight at the 1920 Games, which took place in Antwerp, Belgium, outpointing Canada's Art Prud'homme in the final. At the 1924 Olympics, which took place in Paris, Mallin repeated his success in the middleweight division by outpointing fellow Briton John Elliott on points.

The 2016 Olympic Games saw the introduction of the Val Barker trophy for female participants, of which American Claressa Shields became the first winner. Shields had, for the second consecutive games, won the gold medal in the middleweight division, outpointing Nouchka Fontijn of the Netherlands to take the championship.

It looked like there was no stopping Roman Gonzalez, a fighter who clearly had his foot firmly on the ladder of greatness; he made history at the Forum Inglewood in California in a contest that took place on 10 September 2016 when Gonzalez became the first Nicaraguan to win a world championship in four different weight divisions when he defeated defending title-holder Carlos Cuadras of Mexico for the WBC super-flyweight crown by a twelve-round points decision. Previous world titles held by Gonzalez were the WBA minimumweight, WBA light-flyweight, and the WBC flyweight. It was clear before the fight got underway that the fans were going to see a fight of quality between two class performers. Both fighters entered the ring with undefeated records. Gonzalez had a perfect slate of forty-five wins while Cuadras had a record of thirty-five victories with one draw.

A new British heavyweight champion was duly crowned on 7 October 2016 when Dillian Whyte won the vacant title when opponent Ian Lewison retired in round ten of a scheduled twelve in a bout that took place at the SSE Hydro in Glasgow. This was the first time that a British heavyweight title had been contested in Scotland.

On 9 November 2016, at the age of seventy-six years, two months, and thirty days, Jack Bodell passed away. Bodell was born on 11 August 1940; he was a former British, European, and Commonwealth heavyweight champion. Jack had engaged in seventy-one professional bouts, of which he won fifty-eight and lost thirteen. In that time, Jack fought a number of quality opponents like Henry Cooper (twice), Joe Bugner, Jerry Quarry, Thad Spencer, Brian London, Joe Erskine, Billy Walker, Ray Patterson, Piero Tomasoni, Jose Manuel Urtain, and Danny McAlinden. Bodell was often underrated, but he has the distinction of being the first fighter who boxed in the southpaw stance to win the British heavyweight title. This event took place on 13 October 1969, when Jack outpointed Carl Gizzi over fifteen rounds at the Ice Rink in Nottingham to claim the vacant title Henry Cooper had relinquished.

On 19 November 2016, Claressa Shields made her professional debut at super-middleweight, outpointing fellow American Franchon Crews Dezurn over four rounds at the T-Mobile Arena in Las Vegas. Shields hence became the first female Olympic gold medallist to box for pay. Claressa had twice won gold at middleweight, the first occasion being in London 2012 and then in Rio 2016.

One of Ireland's great amateur boxers, Katie Taylor (the 2012 Olympic games gold medallist) made a successful professional lightweight debut on 26 November 2016 at Wembley Arena. Opponent Karina Kopinska of Poland provided the opposition but was not able to go the full scheduled six rounds when halted in the third session. Taylor looked set to emulate her amateur success in the paid ranks.

Kal Yafai was due to challenge Panama's Luis Concepcion at the Manchester Arena for the WBA world super-flyweight title on 10 December 2016. However, prior to the contest, Concepcion, with a résumé of thirty-five wins with just four defeats, lost the championship on the scales at the weigh-in since he was unable to come in at the stipulated poundage. The bout went ahead for the vacant crown with only Yafai able to take the

Jack Bodell, the first boxer with the
southpaw stance to win the British
heavyweight title, passed away in 2016.
(*Derek Rowe*)

title should he win. After twelve rounds, Yafai did indeed take the victory
over his opponent with an empathic points victory. Yafai entered the ring
undefeated with a record of twenty victories and hence became the first
British boxer to win a world championship in this weight division.

Joseph Parker met Mexican-American opponent Andy Ruiz Jr at the
Spark Arena in Auckland, New Zealand, on 10 December 2016 to contest
the vacant WBO world heavyweight crown. The title had been vacated by
Tyson Fury of the UK. The fans were treated to twelve rounds of competitive
boxing by the two opposing fighters looking to claim the respective
championship. Parker hence won the title by way of points decision. In so
doing, Parker became the first New Zealand-born boxer to win a major
version of the world heavyweight championship. The two boxers entered
the ring with undefeated records: Parker's stood at twenty-one and Ruiz Jr
entered the fray with a slate of twenty-nine. The contest was also the first
world heavyweight title bout to take place in New Zealand.

On 14 January 2017, James DeGale (the IBF world super-middleweight champion) from the UK met Swedish-born, American-based Badou Jack (the world WBC holder of the title) in a unification contest. At the Barclays Center in Brooklyn, New York, the two warriors produced an exciting, hard-hitting contest where both men paid a visit to the canvas and took a count from the referee: Badou went down in the first round and Degale in the twelfth. Both fighters pushed themselves to the very limit and when the bell sounded to end the fight, the decision looked like it was going to be a very close one. The two boxers were well matched. However, the judges duly declared the bout a draw after twelve rounds. Both men therefore kept their versions of the championship.

It was time to get even for Leo Santa Cruz on 28 January 2017 when at the MGM Grand, Las Vegas, when he regained the WBA super world featherweight crown by outpointing holder Carl Frampton of Northern Ireland over twelve rounds. Frampton not only lost his title but his undefeated record, which stood at twenty-three going into the bout. In their previous meeting, which took place on 30 July 2016, Frampton took away Cruz's undefeated slate, which was thirty-two wins with one draw, when he won a twelve-round points verdict to take the respective crown. On this occasion, Cruz returned the compliment.

On 24 February 2017, Welshman Jay Harris outpointed Cameroon-born champion Thomas Essomba over twelve rounds for the Commonwealth flyweight title at York Hall in Bethnal Green, London. By coincidence, on the same date twenty-nine years earlier, Jay's father Peter Harris captured the vacant British featherweight crown at the Afan Lido in Port Talbot, Wales, outpointing Kevin Taylor over twelve rounds.

It looked like a sure-fire win for David Haye (the former holder of the WBA world heavyweight and WBC, WBA, WBO world cruiserweight and European cruiserweight titles) when he stepped inside the ring at 02 Arena (Millenium Doom) in London on 4 March 2017. Haye was to duke it out with reigning WBC world cruiserweight champion Tony Bellew in a contest made at heavyweight. Many experts were of the view that it would be an easy night for Haye, even going as far as to say it was a mismatch. Yet some vied on the size of caution with the view that it would be foolish for Haye to underestimate his opponent. Apart from holding a world title, Bellew was also a former British and Commonwealth light-heavyweight king and former European cruiserweight champion. Bellew had the heart of a lion and in the past, the fighter had shown that whether he win or lose, he was a man who would not quit easily—a quality he revealed in the exciting encounter with Haye. During the early rounds, Bellew withstood the power of Haye and fired back with his own punches. Many who follow the sport know that boxing often offers up a surprise and this encounter was no exception; Bellew emerged a winner when in round six, Haye suffered a ruptured Achilles tendon. Despite the painful injury, Haye bravely fought on until his corner threw the towel in during round eleven of a contest set for twelve. Bellew had added to the history of boxing upsets.

Alejandra Jimenez of Mexico made the first defence of her WBC world female heavyweight title on 1 April 2017 at the Zocalo, Mexico City. All signs indicated that Jimenez would turn back her American challenger Carlette Ewell and remain champion but not without a battle. However, Jimenez exceeded expectations when she defeated Ewell, becoming the first title-holder of this version of championship to register a first-round win in a championship contest scheduled for ten.

Nicola Adams, the double Olympic flyweight gold medallist, started her journey in the professional ranks on 8 April 2017 at the Manchester Arena. Adams showed her class when outpointing Virginia Noemi Carcamo of Argentina over four rounds.

Nicola Adams, the double Olympic gold medallist, started her professional career in 2017.
(*Philip Sharkey*)

On 22 April 2017, Ashley Brace from Wales gave her fans plenty to cheer about when at the Leisure Centre in Ebbw Vale, she impressively stopped Alexandra Vlajk of Hungary in the ninth of a ten-round contest. In so doing, she won the vacant WBC international female bantamweight crown and hence became the first from the UK to win this title. Wales has produced a number of top tier fighters over the years; it had to be wondered at this point if Brace was going to add her name to the illustrative list.

Amanda Serrano of Puerto Rico challenged Dahiana Santana of the Dominican Republic for the vacant WBO female world bantamweight crown on 22 April 2017. The pair met at the Barclays Center in Brooklyn, New York, in a contest set for ten rounds. Santana found that her southpaw opponent had too much for her to handle and was stopped in the eighth stanza. The win by Serrano saw her become the first lady boxer to hold a version of a world championship in five different weight divisions. Serrano previously held the following world crowns: WBO super-bantamweight, WBO, IBA, UBF featherweight, WBO lightweight, and IBF super-featherweight.

One of the biggest fights to be staged in the UK took place on 29 April 2017 at Wembley Stadium in London. A reported number of 90,000 spectators paid to see London's Anthony Joshua not only make his third defence of his IBF world heavyweight crown but contest the vacant WBA super heavyweight and vacant IBO versions of the championship. The fight had the nation and the boxing world gripped. Joshua entered the ring to face former IBF, WBA, WBO, and IBO title-holder Wladimir Klitschko—a vastly more experienced fighter, having taken part in sixty-four bouts (winning sixty and losing four); he had taken part in twenty-eight world title bouts, be it either as a champion or challenger. Joshua in comparison was undefeated in eighteen contests. Both Klitschko and Joshua had won gold medals at the Olympic Games at super heavyweight. Klitschko struck gold at the 1996 Games in Atlanta, defeating Paea Wolfgramm of Tonga while Joshua did the same at the 2012 competition in London, defeating Italy's Roberto Cammarelle. The exciting fight between Joshua and Klitschko gave the fans everything they could ask for with the Ukrainian being floored for a count in round five. Then in round six, Klitschko reminded everyone that he too had punching power when he introduced the Briton to the canvas for the first time in his paid career. Joshua showed that he had a solid chin and could take a punch when he beat the count and fought on. The end came in round eleven of the scheduled twelve-round contest when Joshua found the range and punch to put his opponent down twice more for counts from the referee. Upon rising, Klitschko faced a two-fisted assault from his opponent, forcing him on to the ropes where the referee stopped the contest in favour of Joshua.

At that moment in time, the rival champions were Deontay Wilder (WBC) from the USA and Joseph Parker (WBO) from New Zealand. However, there was no doubting the fact that Joshua was the main man in the division—the fighter who had the global attention.

One had to wonder if George Groves would ever ascend to a world title after three setbacks when challenging for the crown. Groves first came unstuck against fellow Briton Carl Froch on 23 November 2013 at the Phones 4u Arena in Manchester when challenging for the IBF and WBA super-middleweight crown. After making a positive start Groves was stopped in round nine of twelve. A return took place on 31 May 2014, which resulted in yet another heartbreaking defeat for Groves at Wembley Stadium. Froch ensured that Groves would not last the full twelve rounds, hence knocking him out in the eighth to retain the titles. Groves regrouped and put some wins together; once again, he was given a title shot. This time, the man he had to face was Swedish-born title-holder Badou Jack, who was the reigning WBC king. Jack was a good champion and would not be a walkover but those who knew the game tipped the Briton to be successful on his third attempt. At the MGM Grand, at the Grand Garden Arena in Las Vegas, Groves once again found that the fates seemed to be against him when he lost a twelve-round points decision. In many ways, it seemed all over for Groves on the world scene. Yet once again, Groves regrouped, revealing a steely resolve to fight on and after a few more wins, he secured yet another title tilt. The fourth chance came on 27 May 2017 at the Bramall Lane Football Ground, Sheffield, where he was to contest the vacant WBA super-middleweight crown. His opponent was the former holder of this title, Russian-born Fedor Chudinov. This was clearly the last chance for Groves; should he fail on this attempt at the championship, it would clearly be the end of any dreams he may harbour of being a world champ. There was little likelihood of him being presented with a fifth challenge so the pressure was well and truly on George. However, this time, Groves came through, stopping Chudinov in round six of a scheduled twelve-round battle.

On 10 June 2017, Ryan Burnett boxed his way to an exciting twelve-round points decision over England's defending IBF world bantamweight champion Lee Haskins to take the crown. The contest took place at the Odyssey Arena in Belfast, Northern Ireland. In gaining victory, Burnett became the first boxer from Northern Ireland to hold a version of the world bantamweight championship since Wayne McCullough, who reigned has the WBC king from 1995 to 1997.

It looked as if Manny Pacquiao would not only enter Australia as the reigning WBO world welterweight champion but would also leave as the WBO world welterweight champion at the end of his contest. However, a shock was in store for the man from the Philippines. Pacquiao stepped into the battle zone at the Suncorp Stadium in Brisbane, Queensland on 2 July 2017 with a record of fifty-nine victories, six defeats, and two draws. Australian challenger Jeff Horn came armed with a résumé of sixteen wins and one draw. To all and sundry, it looked as if another win for the defending champion was on the cards. In truth, it seemed a routine outing for the champion. After a hard-fought twelve-round battle, the points decision went to Horn. The rival world welterweight champions at that time were Americans Keith Thurman (WBA and WBC) and Errol Spence Jr (IBF).

On 4 August 2017, American Claressa Shields ducked between the ropes at the MGM Grand in Detroit, Michigan to challenge Germany's Nikki Adler for her WBC world female super-middleweight title; also on the line was the vacant IBF crown. In her fourth bout, Shields stopped the undefeated Adler, who was participating in her seventeenth outing in round five of ten to win the titles. In so doing, Shields became the first female Olympic gold medallist to become a professional world champion: Shields won gold at middleweight in the 2012 and 2016 games.

It was a showdown to see who the best super-lightweight in the world was. In a contest that took place on 19 August 2017, American Terence Crawford (the WBC and WBO title-holder) stepped in with Julius Indongo of Namibia (the WBA and IBF world super-lightweight champion). The venue for the battle for global supremacy took place at Pinnacle Bank in Lincoln, Nebraska. Both men were undefeated: Crawford in thirty-one outings and Indongo in twenty-two. Someone had to lose their undefeated record and that someone was Indongo, who was knocked out in the third session of a scheduled twelve-round contest. At that moment in time, Crawford became the only world champion to hold all four versions of the title in his respective weight division.

It was a fight that captured the public's imagination. It took place on 26 August 2017 at the T-Mobile Arena in Las Vegas, Nevada. The two men who shared the ring for the contest were the most accomplished Floyd Mayweather Jr and UFC fighter Ireland's Conor McGregor. Mayweather Jr had come out of retirement to accommodate McGregor, a man who was having his first professional contest. Did McGregor have any chance of defeating Mayweather Jr? The answer was that he did not. However, McGregor lasted into the tenth round of a contest set for twelve when the referee stepped in to end proceedings, giving Floyd the win. The victory gave Mayweather Jr his fiftieth victory, surpassing the undefeated record of forty-nine previously held by former world heavyweight champion Rocky Marciano.

On 8 September 2017, American David Benavidez opposed Romanian Ronald Gavril for the vacant WBC world super-middleweight championship. Benavidez was undefeated in eighteen bouts; Gavril had comprised a record of eighteen wins with one defeat. The contest for the title took place at the Hard Rock Hotel and Casino in Las Vegas, Nevada. At the end of the absorbing twelve-round battle, Benavidez was given the decision on points. On this occasion, Benavidez became the youngest man to win a version of this title at the age of twenty years, eight months, and twenty-two days.